AMA Complete Guide to
MARKETING RESEARCH FOR SMALL BUSINESS

AMA Complete Guide to
MARKETING
RESEARCH
FOR SMALL
BUSINESS

Holly Edmunds

Printed on recyclable paper

AMERICAN
MARKETING
ASSOCIATION

NTC Business Books
a division of *NTC Publishing Group* • Lincolnwood, Illinois USA

Library of Congress Cataloging-in-Publication Data

Edmunds, Holly.
  AMA complete guide to marketing research for small business /
Holly Edmunds.
     p.   cm.
  Includes index.
  ISBN 0–8442–3584–9 (alk. paper)
  1. Marketing research. 2. Small business. I. Title.
HF5415.2.E34 1996
658.8'3—dc20   96–10743
                                     CIP

Published in conjunction with the American Marketing Association,
250 South Wacker Drive, Chicago, Illinois 60606.

Published by National Textbook Company, a division of NTC Publishing Group.
© 1996 by NTC Publishing Group, 4255 West Touhy Avenue,
Lincolnwood (Chicago), Illinois 60646–1975 U.S.A.
Manufactured in the United States of America.

6 7 8 9 0 QB 9 8 7 6 5 4 3 2 1

Dedication

For his support and patience through this effort (and life in general) this book is dedicated to my husband, David.

Contents

Chapter Six
Developing a Winning Telephone Survey   51

Chapter 7
Focus Groups   65

Chapter Eight
Mystery Shopping Programs **87**

Chapter Nine
Quality Control in Market Research **99**

Chapter Ten

Selecting and Working with a Research Vendor

105

Chapter Eleven

"Making or Breaking" Your Research Budget

111

Acknowledgments

Many thanks to my children, James and Rebecca, who had to deal with Mom being locked in her office to work on the manuscript. Thanks also to my editors Rich Hagle and David Bramer for their patience and assistance in this effort.

Chapter One

Defining Your Marketing Research Needs

The need for information is common to all businesses. Without information, business owners would have no basis for making the decisions that affect their business growth and profits. Most small business owners can readily list questions that they want to have answered and issues that they need to resolve. Yet if you ask typical small business owners if they plan to conduct research to get those answers, most will simply shrug and say they cannot afford it or do not have the necessary expertise. Issues are frequently resolved by calling on educated guesswork and past experience.

This book provides alternatives to this hit-or-miss approach to decision making. Although the ideal market research scenario would dictate the use of a specialized research vendor or consultant, this book recognizes that most small businesses have limited funds for research and provides cost-effective market research options. Most of these research studies can be conducted internally without extensive education or experience in market research.

Throughout the text, important terms that might be unfamiliar will appear in **bold type** when they are first mentioned. These terms are defined at the end of each chapter as well as in the glossary at the end of the book. In most cases, detailed explanations of these terms are also provided in the section in which they appear.

When Do You Need Research?

How do you recognize the need for **market research** in your organization? Generally, whenever your company faces questions for which answers are not readily apparent, you should think about conducting some form of research. Consider the following examples:

- You own a successful restaurant and you are thinking about opening a second location, but you are not sure about the best site.
- Customer complaints are on the rise, but you cannot identify the main trouble spot.
- You wonder whether your advertisements are producing the desired effect.
- A new store has opened a few blocks away and is directly competing with your store on a price basis. You want to determine the best means of countering this potential threat to your customer base.
- You are considering a substantial change to a current product or service, but you are unsure how your customers will react or how well the move will serve to attract new customers (if at all).

These are just a few of the multitude of potential situations in which research can help you make the best decision and, accordingly, save money that might otherwise be wasted by relying on guesswork and heading in the wrong direction.

 Research does not make decisions for you. Instead, it provides you with sufficient information to allow *you* to make informed decisions.

Two Major Research Categories: Primary and Secondary

The type of research you will conduct depends on a number of variables, including when the results are needed, what objectives need to be met, and the budget that is available (however limited). There are two main categories of market research: primary and secondary. See Chapter 2 for an extensive discussion of research methods.

Secondary Research

Secondary research consists of gathering data that has already been compiled for any purpose other than the research question currently being considered. For instance, you might look up demographic information such as age and income ranges for a specific city in U.S. Census reports. Or you might develop sales trend graphs based on numbers obtained from your company's sales receipts.

 The efficient (and thrifty) researcher avoids "reinventing the wheel" whenever possible.

Many small businesses are unaware of the reams of information to which they have easy access, often at little or no cost. Depending on your **research objectives,** consider the secondary resources before designing your own market study. Some possible information sources to consider include the following:

- U.S. Census reports
- Data from trade associations or professional organizations
- Reports from local Chambers of Commerce
- Internal information such as sales or service records and warranty information
- Articles in business periodicals

You might even be able to glean new insights from previous studies done internally that touch on the topic you are interested in. A word of caution is in order, however, concerning *any* secondary research materials:

 Old studies yield old results.

If a survey is more than two years old, consider it history and avoid using it for current decision-making purposes. Even two-year-old data might be misleading, depending on the subject matter and the rate at which changes occur in your company, industry, and marketplace.

When in doubt about what secondary information is available, ask for help. Failing to ask questions now can lead to wasted research later. Reference librarians at public or university libraries are frequently a good starting point. Local Small Business Information Centers run by the Commerce Department can also assist by identifying the best report to meet your needs. In addition, the Internet, a worldwide network of computer networks, now makes available many research reports directly from a computer in your home or place of business.

Primary Research

Once your search for secondary information is complete, you are ready to decide whether you still need additional information. If secondary research is too general or nonexistent for your specific objectives, you should consider conducting **primary research—** studies that you design yourself. Primary research is the focus of this book.

Although primary research can be an intimidating prospect, you might actually be conducting primary research already and simply calling it by another name. Do you regularly collect and update customer information (such as age, address, and product preferences)? Do you consistently ask callers how they found out about your store or business and then track their responses? These are just two examples of how small businesses gather and compile information. This book will guide you in reviewing and improving the research skills you have already developed through experience.

Defining Your Objectives

Before you decide how to conduct a study (the research **methodology**), you need to determine exactly what it is that you are trying to find out. Start by making a "wish list" of things that you would like to learn from your research.

Determine first what you need answers *for*—once you get results, what purpose will they serve? Anticipate the end result of your research work.

You can use Worksheet 1–1 to gain practice in developing sound market research objectives. Consider a hypothetical restaurant that is experiencing steadily increasing business. Opening a second location could result in increased name recognition and profits. But the business owner is not certain which locations will be most attractive to current and potential customers. In the worksheet, imagine yourself as the restaurateur and list at least five things you would want to learn about any new locations being considered.

Worksheet 1–1

Instructions: List at least five research objectives for a business owner who is opening another site.

1. _____
   _____

2. _____
   _____

3. _____
   _____

4. _____
   _____

5. _____
   _____

The worksheet provides space for five objectives, but there are actually unlimited numbers of issues that could be addressed through market research. A sample of the restaurant owner's initial list of objectives might include the following:

1. Determine income levels and age ranges of current customers.
2. Locate similar age/income groups within county lines.
3. Determine the percentage of current customers who visit for lunch versus dinner.
4. Determine the strengths and weaknesses of the current location.
5. Choose the best promotion(s) to draw customers to the new location.
6. Consider the possible loss of current customers to the new location **(cannibalization).**
7. Examine the competition around the potential site(s).
8. Look at **efficiencies of scale** involved with operating two locations. (Will some expenses be combined, providing greater cost-effectiveness, such as payroll management, food purchases, or training?)
9. Test **target market** interest levels regarding a restaurant *(your restaurant specifically)* in the potential location(s).

After brainstorming to generate an extensive list of possible issues to be researched, the business owner will need to focus on those issues that will most strongly influence the success of the new location and eliminate the peripheral issues.

Of the issues or questions that remain, not all are candidates for a full research effort. Some could be addressed using existing internal sources of information, and some could be researched at the library. (See Chapter 2 for more information about secondary research.)

You can use Worksheet 1–2 to record ideas for alternative sources of information that could potentially resolve the nine research objectives listed above. You should narrow the original list to three objectives that require a formal research effort.

Worksheet 1–2

Instructions: Narrow down the original nine objectives to the three most important objectives that are appropriate for primary research. For each point not included, suggest alternative sources for that information.

Objectives for Primary Research

1. _____

2. _____

3. _____

Other Data Sources for Remaining Objectives

1. _____

2. _____

3. _____

4. _____

5. _____

6. _____

Of the nine objectives, the following six can be effectively resolved without a formal study:

- Objective 2: Age and income data for potential sites could be obtained through U.S. Census reports.

- Objective 3: Internal records can show the relative percentages of lunch and dinner patronage.

- Objective 5: It is probably premature to evaluate promotions for a new location until an actual site is selected and a target market is identified.

- Objective 6: ZIP codes of current customers (if already available on your records) could help to determine whether they would be likely to visit the new location and stop patronizing the current one.

- Objective 7: Some information regarding the number of competitors in selected areas is available through local Chambers of Commerce. Greater detail is best obtained by eating at area competitors' restaurants yourself to evaluate pricing, atmosphere, service, and quality.

- Objective 8: Cost savings issues would require an internal financial analysis rather than research.

From the original nine objectives, ultimately the following three remain as potential market research objectives:

- Objective 1: Determine income levels and age ranges of the current customer base.
- Objective 4: Determine the strengths and weaknesses of the current location.
- Objective 9: Test target market interest levels regarding a restaurant in the potential locations.

Now you are ready to move on to selecting a research methodology—how to get this information.

Terms to Remember

Cannibalization   In a marketing sense, a firm losing customers from one of its locations to another

Efficiencies of scale   Cost savings that arise from combining the operations or expenses of two divisions, purchasing in larger quantities, etc.

Market research   The process of gathering and analyzing information about the market in order to provide information for decision making

Methodology   The means by which a study is conducted (e.g., mail surveys, mystery shops, focus groups)

Primary research   Research designed specifically to address the research objective(s) currently being addressed

Research objectives   What the researcher wants to find out from the research study

Secondary research   Gathering data that was compiled previously by another organization or internally for a different research objective

Target market   The segment of the market or the group of potential customers, to which sales efforts are directed

Chapter Two

Selecting the Optimum Research Methodology

Types of Primary Research

Primary research can be broken down into two general categories: **quantitative research** and **qualitative research.** Non-researchers are usually more familiar with quantitative research, which consists of **surveys** or any other type of study in which the results are in the form of hard numbers or percentages. Both quantitative and qualitative methods must follow established procedures to yield reliable results. Because qualitative methods allow for more subjective interpretation, different researchers will produce different findings from the same study. In contrast, a well-designed quantitative study will produce the same findings no matter who conducts the research.

Quantitative Research

All of us at one time or another have completed a survey asking, for example, how satisfied we are with our financial institution's customer service or how well we like the new car we recently purchased. And, most likely, you have been contacted at least once by a telephone research interviewer who wanted to ask you questions about your personal computer choice or favorite television show. These surveys are conducted using a specific questionnaire and (if done correctly) using a predetermined technique to **sample** (select) potential survey **respondents.** Survey sampling will be discussed in greater detail in Chapter 3.

When a survey is completed, the responses to each question are **tabulated** (tallied) and percentages are figured to determine answers to your research objectives. For example, 25 percent of the respondents prefer to bank near where they work; 15 percent have two separate checking accounts in their households, etc. Providing that a large enough number of persons have responded to the survey, the results of the survey will be accurate enough to use in decision making. An example of tabulated results is shown in Exhibit 2–1.

Exhibit 2–1

Database Table Examples

Q15 What is the main reason you chose to do business with Commerce Bank?

	Total	Male	Female	18–35	36–55	65+
Responses	300	150	150	123	101	76
Close to home	32%	42%	23%	28%	25%	48%
	97	63	34	35	25	37
Recommendation	29%	16%	43%	41%	33%	7%
	88	24	64	50	33	5
Best deposit rates	17%	18%	15%	12%	30%	7%
	50	27	23	15	30	5
Other	22%	24%	19%	19%	12%	38%
	65	36	29	23	13	29

Qualitative Research

Qualitative methods are generally less structured than surveys or other quantitative studies. However, they are no less valid as a source of information for business decisions, provided that researchers adhere to quality-control guidelines. Major types of qualitative methods include focus groups, one-on-one interviews, and mystery shopping.

Focus Groups

The most frequently used qualitative method is the **focus group,** a discussion group conducted by a moderator and designed to create an ongoing conversation about one or more issues related to a general topic. The size of the groups is small, usually 8–10 participants. Therefore, focus groups do not provide hard figures or percentages as surveys do. Rather, they provide a flow of input and customer quotations about the subject being discussed. Usually two or more groups are conducted to allow for comparisons of participants' opinions and reactions.

One-on-One Interviews

In **one-on-one interviews,** an interviewer meets with one participant at a time and conducts less structured "surveys" or a conversation similar to that of a focus group. This type of qualitative research is useful for addressing many types of research objectives, such as testing advertising concepts or trying out a new product when people need to see or test something or to give an explanation that would be too lengthy or technical over the phone. One-on-one interviews are also frequently used as a means of gathering preliminary information to be used in developing a larger quantitative study.

Another form of the one-on-one study is an **intercept interview.** In these cases, an interviewer stops consumers on the street or in a mall, either at random or, for example, as they leave a specific store, and conducts a brief in-person survey.

Mystery Shopping

Another frequently used qualitative research methodology is a **mystery shop program.** Mystery shops, most simply described, involve interviewers or "shoppers," as they are called in this study type, going into a retail store, for example, and pretending to be customers. They might make a purchase, return an earlier purchase, or simply inquire about a specific product or service. Upon exiting the store, they complete detailed evaluation forms based on their "shop" experiences. A number of shops are generally completed to allow for an overall evaluation of the store's (or stores') performance.

Frequently, competitors' stores are also shopped to allow for service comparisons. Shops are used to ensure quality controls, provide feedback for training departments, and often as part of employee incentive programs. Although reports on shop results often provide what appear as hard numbers in table format, shops should be considered qualitative in nature because they are not statistically replicable and often comprise small sample sizes. Chapter 8 presents more detail about mystery shops.

Choosing the Right Methodology

Selecting the right methodology to meet your needs depends on several factors. Some types of research studies are more costly or take longer to complete than others. A low budget or tight time restrictions could in part determine what your research options will be. Consider the following questions before reviewing the possible methods described in later chapters:

- What specifically do you need to learn from this study?
- What objectives have you defined? (See Chapter 1.)
- What is available in terms of sample?
- Do you have lists of customers?
- Can you obtain lists of potential survey respondents through a trade association, for example?

- Do you need a very specifically defined respondent that might require purchasing a list from a **list broker** or list distribution firm?
- What are your expected budgetary and time constraints?

These selection criteria are provided based on the assumption that you and/or a staff member would be responsible for designing, coordinating, and analyzing the results of the study. If you are working with a research vendor, these same criteria will affect the feasibility and affordability of the project.

The following criteria are not listed in order of their importance. Rather, they should all be taken into consideration when determining which type of research study will best meet your own needs.

Timing

When you need the results of a study can affect which methodology you select for your research. If you have minimal time limitations, a mail survey will work fine; it typically will require eight weeks or more to conduct including preparation and analysis. If quicker turnaround is necessary, however, a telephone survey would be preferable. This could be completed within one month versus the two required for a mail survey provided sample and interviewers are readily available. Focus groups also require about a one-month time span from start to finish, but before selecting this methodology be certain that your objectives warrant qualitative rather than quantitative research.

Budget

Your budget will probably play a role in the research decision. Telephone surveys tend to be more costly to administer than mail surveys. If you conduct focus groups, the cost of the room and refreshments may not be too "pricey," but you cannot forget the "co-op" or compensation for the focus group participants. When planning a research study, you need to be aware of *all* possible costs associated with the various methodologies.

Ease of Project Coordination

Your choice of methodology may have to be made in conjunction with how much time you have to coordinate the project. While a telephone survey may yield quicker results for you, you may not have adequate time to coordinate interviewers internally and too small of a budget to conduct interviews through a research vendor. Given your time constraints, you may choose to conduct a mail survey which would require only upfront design, printing and mailing and later the analysis.

Research Objectives

The methodology selected is very dependent upon the research objectives you have determined for your study. If you need to get input from customers regarding several advertising concepts which they need to view, a focus group will serve best. If, however, you want to set a baseline for a quality assurance program with ratings related to customers' satisfaction levels, you will need to conduct some form of quantitative study, by mail or by phone.

List Availability

You cannot survey customers without lists of the customers to contact. (You could try calling at random and screening to locate customers but this could be costly.) Likewise, a mail survey is difficult to conduct without access to address listings. Your research is limited by your access to lists as well as the accuracy of those lists. If you have mailing addresses for your customers, but not telephone numbers, then by default you will probably conduct a mail survey. For non-customers, lists are easier to come by, as discussed in Chapter 3.

 Do not sacrifice quality by rushing a study or by automatically doing it as cheaply as possible. Slipshod research efforts are expensive if you make the wrong decision based on sloppy, incorrect results.

Terms to Remember

Focus group A research discussion group conducted by a moderator and designed to create an ongoing conversation about one or more issues related to a general topic

Intercept interviews A research method in which interviewers stop consumers on the street or in a mall to conduct in-person interviews

List broker Firm that sells lists covering an extensive variety of detailed breakdowns such as geographic location, age, profession, etc.

Mystery shops program Studies in which interviewers go into an establishment under guise of being customers or potential customers to test that company's service and sales efforts

One-on-one interviews Less structured "surveys" or discussions conducted in person by an interviewer with one participant at a time

Qualitative research Less structured research methods (e.g., focus groups or one-on-one interviews) whose results are subject to interpretation

Quantitative research Structured research methods designed to provide statistically valid results in the form of numbers and percentages

Respondent A person who completes a questionnaire by phone or mail

Sample The lists of people or businesses who will be contacted to participate in a given study

Survey Research study using a questionnaire to collect data from respondents via telephone or mail contact

Tabulate To tally survey responses

Chapter **Three**

Gathering Sample for Your Research

The success of any market research effort depends as much on identifying survey respondents as it does on developing worthwhile survey questions. This chapter addresses four basic guidelines for ensuring that sufficient numbers of the right people are answering your questions:

1. Identify your target respondents.
2. Determine the statistically correct sample size for the population.
3. Take into account the nonresponse rate.
4. Consider a range of possible sources.

Determining Your Target Respondents

The respondents needed for your study are selected in response to the information you need to uncover. Do you need to speak with hands-on users of your product/service or the purchase decision maker, or both? Depending on the topic, the answers you get from each could vary significantly. If you are talking about price, who could best respond to your questions? Most likely it will be the purchaser. But for questions regarding product/service quality, the actual user would probably provide the most valuable, knowledge-able input. Following are some of the target groups to consider for a survey or focus group project:

- Users of your product/service
- Potential customers/users
- Business owners
- Consumers (in general)
- Registered voters
- Residents of a specific area
- Your employees
- Your competitors (anonymously, of course!)

Determining the Statistically Correct Sample Size

In market research, *sample* refers to the set of people who will be contacted to participate in a given study. The overall group of people or businesses from which you select your sample is called the **population.** If you are calling residents of your city, all persons residing within the city limits (usually adults over the age of 18) comprise the total population for your survey. In the survey, how-ever, you will interview only a selected sample of this population. To be representative of the population, an adequate number of interviews (or written surveys) must be completed for your results to be statistically correct.

Confidence Levels

Sample sizes are generally based on reliability statistics within certain **confidence levels.** In other words, how confident do you need to be that results will fall within a specific range or reliability statistic? The research industry generally looks for "plus or minus 5.5 percent at the 95 percent confidence level." This means that if you repeat the study in the same way with the same **survey sampling** procedure, the survey responses will fall within plus or minus 5.5 percent of those given in the initial version of the survey, and you can be 95 percent confident that these findings are accurate.

This text is not intended to delve into statistics, but, for internal purposes, a basic guideline is to aim for a **base** of 300 completed surveys for most populations. If you intend to break the resulting data out by various criteria, such as gender, age, or county and conduct detailed analysis by these segments, you will require a larger overall sample size. If you work with an outside vendor to conduct your survey, your project manager can help you determine the appropriate number of surveys. If you want greater detail concerning the statistical reliability of survey samples, most statistics and market research textbooks offer detailed explanations.

If you are conducting a mystery shop, the sample size will not be as large, because it is not feasible to hire so many shoppers. Likewise, if you are surveying customers coming into your store on a given day or weekend, you might not get 300 completed surveys. Because a base of 300 is not always possible, it is important to recognize the statistical limitations of any base smaller than 300. In other words, you should not base major decisions on the information gained from 10 or 15 surveys.

Random Selection

When conducting telephone surveys, sample is usually selected randomly, either from a list (for example, of customers) or a random-digit dialing process. Vendors with large banks of telephone interviewers frequently use random-digit dialing. For your own purposes, it is simplest (and still appropriate) to select every *n*th (say, every fifth) name from your list to contact.

Depending on the extent of your telephone survey, you might consider purchasing a prerandomized list of telephone numbers from your local telephone company. These lists are generally sold by groups of a thousand contacts and can be drawn by telephone prefix, city, etc. These lists are useful, for example, for recruiting focus groups or surveying noncustomers to identify potential users of your product or service.

Accounting for the Nonresponse Rate

Researchers should always order more sample than they anticipate needing. Not every person contacted by phone or mail for a survey will respond. There is *always* a certain **nonresponse rate** inherent in any market research study, so it is important to have an abundance of sample available. A good rule of thumb for telephone surveys is about an eight-to-one ratio—eight names on the list for every one completed questionnaire expected. Plan on even larger sample lists if you will be contacting very specialized respondents, such as high-level executives who might be difficult to reach on a one-to-one basis.

Considering Potential List Sources

Research vendors are usually willing to obtain lists for you, but inquire first to see whether this service comes at an additional cost. It is frequently less expensive to obtain the lists yourself. Lists for telephone or mail surveys can also be purchased through list brokers, firms that rent lists covering an extensive variety of detailed breakdowns, such as by age, geographic location, profession, ownership of specific car models, hobbies, etc. List brokers can also provide lists of businesses based on a large selection of prescreened criteria, including the size of the business, number of employees, Standard Industrial Classification (SIC) code, and so on. As with the lists obtained through telephone companies, minimum orders are required, with pricing based on the number of names ordered. Such firms can usually be found under "mailing lists" in a Yellow Pages telephone directory.

Assume that a restaurateur wants to look for potential catering customers, specifically among businesses that require catering at their sites for large-scale functions (100 guests or more), such as special parties or shareholders' meetings. The business owner would, of course, need to speak with representatives from larger companies with on-site conference facilities. In Worksheet 3–1, list at least four sources of sample to conduct a brief survey of these businesses to determine their needs.

Provided a budget is available, a list broker or telephone service provider would both present viable options for sample. For example, the restaurateur would request companies occupying office building space with X amount of square footage and with 500 or more employees. Another option would be Chamber of Commerce directories, which typically provide some details regarding the size of the businesses represented in their memberships. The library also maintains a wide variety of different types of business directories that could prove useful in compiling sample. Some such directories are available in an electronic format to allow sorting by ZIP code or business type. When surveying businesses, do not overlook the Yellow Pages as another possible source of business listings.

Terms to Remember

Base Total number of responses to a given survey question; also the total number of completed surveys or shops in a research project

Confidence level The level or percentage of confidence you need to have that your survey results will fall within a specific range of reliability

Nonresponse rate Percentage of contacts on the sample list that do not respond to a survey

Population The overall group from which a survey's sample is selected

Research vendor A professional research company typically offering a variety of market research services, including focus groups, surveys, and mystery shop programs

Survey sampling The process of using specific criteria to select a group of contacts to be surveyed

Chapter Four

Basic Questionnaire Design

Quantitative studies such as mail and telephone surveys and certain qualitative studies such as mystery shop programs require the use of a **questionnaire.** In this chapter, you will learn how to develop your own questionnaire using a simple step-by-step process.

 The keys to a good questionnaire are that it relate directly to your objectives for the study and that it be made as clear and concise as possible.

To provide more visual examples in terms of questionnaire design, we will continue to use the example of the restaurateur from Chapter 1. The owner of Tony's Restaurant has decided to conduct two surveys to obtain the information needed to decide whether to pursue a second location for the business. For the moment, assume that sample has been obtained and that the methodologies have been selected.

A questionnaire will be handed out to customers visiting the current location during a time period to be determined. Customers responding will be given a two-for-one meal certificate as an incentive to participate. A mail survey will be conducted with the general public of the metropolitan area in which the business now operates and in which the second location is being considered. For now, we will concentrate solely on developing the questionnaire for the customer version of the survey. Following is a list of the steps to follow when constructing a questionnaire:

1. Make a "wish list."
2. Prepare an outline.
3. Develop the questionnaire wording.
4. Design the questionnaire format.
5. Prepare for survey analysis.

Making a Wish List

Making a wish list for a questionnaire is similar to the procedure used to determine objectives for deciding whether to conduct a research study. This is an easier task, however, because you will use the original research objectives as guidelines for choosing the questions for the questionnaire.

Following are the three research goals for Tony's Restaurant from Chapter 1:

1. Determine income levels and age ranges of current customer base.
2. Determine current strengths and weaknesses of the current location.
3. Test target market interest levels regarding a restaurant in the potential locations.

Put yourself in the business owner's position for a little while. What types of questions would you ask to get information that would meet the preceding objectives? Use Worksheet 4–1 to list questions you would ask *customers* in order to get the information you need to make your decision. Note that these questions need not be in any particular order, nor do you need to format them as they would appear in the actual questionnaire. This simply provides a starting point for the questionnaire.

Worksheet 4–1

Instructions: Under each objective, list at least three potential questions to ask in a questionnaire. Consider all the various ways to obtain information that could help in making the decision about a second location for Tony's Restaurant.

1. Determine income levels and age ranges of the current customer base.

   _____

   _____

   _____

   _____

   _____

2. Determine the strengths and weaknesses of the current location.

   _____

   _____

   _____

   _____

   _____

   _____

3. Test target market interest levels regarding a restaurant in the potential locations.

   _____

   _____

   _____

   _____

   _____

   _____

Compare your lists of potential questions with the questions that follow. You might have thought of additional questions or omitted some of those shown here. This does not necessarily mean that your questions are incorrect. Be sure, however, as we move further into the development stages, that you reevaluate your questions to determine which are actually necessary to obtain pertinent information and which would provide data that are merely "nice to know."

 The more questions involved in a survey, the greater the expense related to analysis—in terms of either funds paid to an outside vendor or your own time and effort.

Review the following questions to get a sense of the immense scope of possible ways to elicit a given piece of information:

1. **Determine income levels and age ranges of the current customer base.**
   - What is the customer's age?
   - When visiting the current location, how many people does the customer bring along?
   - What are the ages of the people the customer brings?
   - What was the customer's household income (before taxes) for the previous year?

2. **Determine the strengths and weaknesses of the current location.**
   - How often does the customer visit the current location?
   - What time of day does the customer usually come in (or for which meal)?
   - Does the customer have any difficulties finding parking?
   - Is it easy to get into the parking lot/facility?
   - How far does the customer usually travel to get to the current location?
   - Does he or she usually drive, walk, or take public transit to the restaurant?
   - Where does the customer work?

- Where does the customer live?
- What is the main reason the customer chooses to dine at this restaurant (e.g., service, food, selection, price, location)?
- Where else does the customer dine frequently (i.e., restaurants visited more than once a month)?
- Where are those restaurants located?
- Why does he or she choose to go to those restaurants?
- What does the customer think are the strengths and weaknesses of the restaurant?

3. **Test target market interest levels regarding a restaurant in the potential locations.**

- How long (in minutes rather than miles) does it take the customer to reach each of the potential restaurant sites from home? From work?
- Does the customer perceive any of these locations to be more convenient for his or her needs than the current location? Why or why not?
- If the restaurant were located at the current location in addition to any of the potential sites, which location would the customer visit most often? On average, how often would the customer go there per month?
- [If a location was selected *other than* the current location] Would the customer still go occasionally to the original location? How often?
- [If none of the locations are considered convenient] Where would the customer prefer the restaurant to be located? How often would the customer visit said location?

Outlining: Go with the Flow

Once you have developed a general list of questions, you need to put them in an order that will give the questionnaire a smooth flow. It would be very confusing for respondents to answer questions thrown together randomly, such as first giving their age, then telling where they would like the restaurant to relocate, and then going back to describe why they go to the current location.

The simplest way for anyone, experienced researcher or novice, to make sense out of the rough question list is to create either an outline or a **flowchart.** With the outline method, questions are placed in the order you plan to place them in the questionnaire (usually in abbreviated form). Exhibit 4–1 provides the initial portion of a questionnaire outline for the restaurant owner's study.

Screening questions, asked to ensure that respondents meet your qualifications (e.g., head of household, X number of purchases per month) should be asked at the beginning of the questionnaire. **Demographic questions,** which are generally of a more personal nature (e.g., age, income, education level, gender), should be asked at the end of the questionnaire and worded carefully to avoid offending respondents.

Exhibit 4–1

First Section of Questionnaire Outline

   I. Survey Introduction
      A. Who is sponsoring the survey
      B. Purpose of survey
  II. Number of times been to Tony's Restaurant?
      A. First time
         1. How initially heard of it?
      B. Two or more times
 III. Main reason chose Tony's?
  IV. (Usually) come from work or home?
   V. How far to get there?
  VI. Rate importance of issues about restaurant selection (1–5 scale)
      A. 1–2 rating
         1. Why low rating given?
      B. 3–5 rating

With the flowchart method (Exhibit 4–2), each proposed survey question is drawn in a little box. Arrows are drawn to and from each box to represent a direction or **skip pattern** in the questionnaire. You are basically creating a visual diagram of what your questionnaire should look like. The questions need to be put in an order that would make sense to someone who has to read the questionnaire and respond according to your directions.

Exhibit 4–2

First Section of Questionnaire Flowchart

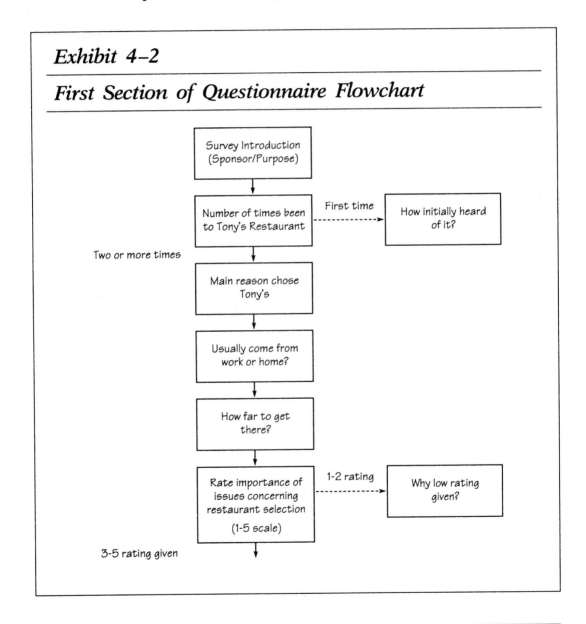

Exhibits 4–1 and 4–2 obviously provide only a very small portion of what the completed outline would look like, but they do give you a starting point and a general sense of how to organize your questions. By visually reviewing the questionnaire in this outline format or with a flowchart diagram, you can most easily determine when a respondent should skip a specific question.

Once the outline or flowchart is complete, ask someone to answer the questions in the order you have placed them. Does the order make sense? Are you missing questions that would cover all possible responses to the outline you have developed? Make revisions accordingly on your diagram or outline before actually completing the formal questionnaire. Now that you have fine-tuned your question order, you are ready to put together the actual questionnaire.

Developing the Questionnaire Wording

Given your survey flowchart or outline, you are prepared to put the outline into questionnaire format. Proper wording of the questions is crucial to your project. If you ask questions in the wrong manner, you could potentially bias your respondents, thereby obtaining incorrect data. If you are insensitive in your wording, respondents might refuse to answer certain questions altogether or possibly even refuse to participate in the survey at all. Consider, for example, the question wordings in Worksheet 4–2. Which question in each set would be the most appropriate?

The preferred wordings for these examples would be 1b, 2c, 3b, and 4a. These are not necessarily the only ways to word the questions, but they are good ways of doing so.

Look again at the questions in Worksheet 4–2. The goal of the questionnaire developer is to ask questions in the least offensive manner possible. Assume for a moment that you are conducting an interview with a person who had dropped out of high school in his or her junior year. Now, years later, this person may regret that decision and not be comfortable discussing it. You, on the other hand, need to learn about respondents' education backgrounds to develop a new advertising campaign. You want to ask this sensitive

Worksheet 4–2

1. **Age:**

   a. How old are you? _____

   b. Into which of the following categories does your age fall?

      21–30, 31–40, 41–50 _____

   c. In what year were you born? _____

2. **Income:**

   a. What was your current year income? _____

   b. How much did you earn last year? _____

   c. Was your current year income above or below $25,000?_____

3. **Education:**

   a. Did you graduate from college?_____

   b. What was the last level of education you had the opportunity to

      complete? _____

   c. What was your last year of school?

      12th grade, bachelor's degree, advanced degree _____

4. **Ad awareness:**

   a. What specifically do you recall from the perfume ad? _____

      _____

      _____

      _____

      _____

      _____

   b. Do you recall the perfume ad with the sunset scene?_____

   c. Did you see the sunset in any of the perfume ads? _____

question in a polite manner which will encourage an honest response. In the preceding worksheet, item 3b seems less accusatory; they may not have had the "opportunity" to complete high school. Be aware of how questions of this type might sound to the respondents during an interview. You want to sound concerned, not invasive.

It is also important to provide the respondents (or, in the case of telephone surveys, the interviewers) with clear instructions to ensure that questions are answered correctly. Exhibit 4–3 shows the portion of the restaurant questionnaire developed using the outline in Exhibit 4–1.

The questionnaire development procedure is similar for mail and telephone surveys. There are, however, aspects of these types of projects that vary. The procedure for conducting mail surveys is covered in Chapter 5, and telephone surveys are detailed in Chapter 6.

Designing the Questionnaire Format

The type of question asked, like the wording of the question, is also important in developing a questionnaire. Consider the following options and decide which might best provide the answers you need to use in your decision-making process.

Open-ended versus Closed-ended Questions

Open-ended questions are questions that allow respondents to provide detailed answers in their own words. They encourage detailed responses, which later are usually coded to combine with like responses. **Closed-ended questions** require specific responses to be selected: yes, no, one or more of several possible responses, or a numerical rating.

Single-Response versus Multiple-Response Questions

Single-response questions are questions that allow respondents to give only one possible response, such as yes or no. **Multiple-response questions** allow respondents to select one or more answers

Exhibit 4–3

First Section of Questionnaire: Tony's Restaurant Customer Survey

Date: _____ / _____ / _____

Tony's Restaurant is considering opening a second location. To identify the site that would best serve our clientele, we are conducting a brief survey of our customers. Please take a few minutes to answer this questionnaire. All of your responses will be kept confidential. When you turn in your completed questionnaire, our cashier will provide you with a 2-for-1 coupon for your next visit. Thank you!

Q1 Approximately how many times have you dined at Tony's during the past 12 months? [CHECK ONE RESPONSE ONLY BELOW]

( ) This is the first time ——> [CONTINUE TO Q2]

( ) 2–5 times ——> [SKIP TO Q3]

( ) 6–10 times ——> [SKIP TO Q3]

( ) 11 times or more ——> [SKIP TO Q3]

Q2 [ANSWER ONLY IF THIS IS YOUR FIRST VISIT]

How did you first hear about Tony's? [CHECK ONE RESPONSE ONLY]

( ) Newspaper ad

( ) Radio ad

( ) Friend/family member/business associate recommended it

( ) Received coupon in the mail

( ) Drove by and saw it

( ) Other [SPECIFY: _____]

( ) Do not recall

——> [SKIP TO Q4] <——

Q3 What is the *main* reason you choose to dine at Tony's? [CHECK ONE REASON ONLY BELOW]

( ) Reasonable prices

( ) Good food

( ) Friendly staff

(Continued)

Exhibit 4–3

( ) Menu selection

( ) Close to home

( ) Close to work

( ) Coupons are available

( ) My friends/family like to eat here

( ) Other [SPECIFY:_____]

Q4 Do you *usually* (or, if this is your first time, did you) come to Tony's from home or from work? [CHECK ONE ONLY BELOW]

( ) Home

( ) Work

( ) Other [SPECIFY:_____]

Q5 And how far do you typically travel to get to Tony's? [CHECK ONE ONLY BELOW]

( ) Less than one mile

( ) 1–2 miles

( ) 3–4 miles

( ) 5–10 miles

( ) 11–20 miles

( ) Over 20 miles

Q6 On a rating scale of one to five, where one means "not at all important" and five means "very important," please rate how important each of the following aspects are to you personally when selecting a restaurant. [CIRCLE ONE RESPONSE PER ITEM]

	Not at all Important				Very Important
a. Atmosphere	1	2	3	4	5
b. Price	1	2	3	4	5
c. Location	1	2	3	4	5
d. Good food	1	2	3	4	5
e. Menu selection	1	2	3	4	5
f. Service	1	2	3	4	5

to the questions (e.g., "Which of the following ads have you seen in the past month? [CHECK ALL THAT APPLY]").

Rankings versus Ratings

Ranking questions ask respondents to place a number of items in rank order (e.g., by importance or preference). Each item has only one number applied to it; none can repeat a number already assigned. If rankings are used, try to keep lists short to keep respondents' confusion to a minimum. Ranking questions should be avoided in telephone surveys if at all possible. Also note that rankings should not be averaged in your analysis.

Rating questions ask respondents to rate items based, for example, on importance, likelihood to purchase, or quality of service. Respondents are provided with a definition of the scale (e.g., 1 means "poor" and 5 means "excellent") and are asked to rate one or more items or statements using that scale. Different items can be given the same rating number, and ratings can be averaged in your analysis. In most cases, it is recommended that odd-point rating scales be used (1–5 or 1–7 are frequently used). Occasionally, even-point scales are used to prevent respondents from taking the "middle of the road" approach that is available with an average rating of 3 in a 5-point scale or 4 in a 7-point scale.

Preparing for Survey Analysis

Once your questionnaire is designed, take a moment to think ahead to how the data will be compiled. If you are using an outside vendor for data processing, check with your vendor *before* you print copies of the questionnaire. The vendor might need specific information on the questionnaire, such as card columns to be used by data entry staff.

Also, look at your questionnaire carefully and ask yourself how the data will be tabulated. Will you need answers to questions based on respondents' age, income, or number of visits to your establishment? If so, make sure these questions are included to allow cross-tabulations later. (Refer to Chapter 5 for more detail about data tabulation.)

Terms to Remember

Closed-ended questions   Questions that require specific responses to be selected, such as "yes" or "no," one or more of several possible multiple-choice responses or a numerical rating

Demographic questions   Questions about respondents, such as age, income, education level, gender and ethnic background, typically used in cross-tabs to provide more meaningful analysis of survey results

Flowchart   A visual diagram used in questionnaire design that indicates each survey question and its related skip pattern

Multiple-response questions   Questions that allow respondents to select one or more responses

Open-ended questions   Questions that allow respondents to write out or respond with detailed answers in their own words

Questionnaire   A survey instrument designed to gather data in a research survey by posing pertinent questions to respondents by phone or mail

Ranking questions   Questions that ask respondents to place a number of items in order by importance, preference, etc.

Rating questions   Questions that ask respondents to assign values (or ratings) from a predetermined scale to a series of items or statements

Screening questions   Questions asked to ensure that survey respondents meet qualifications for the sample

Single-response questions   Questions that allow respondents to give only one possible response

Skip pattern   Part of a questionnaire's format such that, if a certain response is given, the respondent is asked to jump ahead or "skip" to a specified question

Chapter Five

Guidelines for Effective Mail Surveys

Drawbacks of Mail Surveys

Before reviewing the guidelines for conducting mail surveys, it is advisable to be aware of common problems associated with this particular methodology in terms of schedule and accuracy.

Mail surveys are typically a bit less expensive to conduct than telephone surveys, but they are also frequently more time-consuming to set up. In addition to questionnaire development and obtaining or compiling sample for the study, project set-up for mail surveys involves printing hundreds (or, in some cases, thousands) of questionnaires and cover letters, possibly arranging for incentives (to be discussed later), providing postage-paid return envelopes, and, if incoming results are slow to filter back to you, arranging for a follow-up mailing to potential respondents.

Another major drawback to mail surveys is the length of time that passes from the initial survey mailing date until the final cutoff date for receipt of the completed questionnaires. Four to six weeks can pass before enough surveys are available for coding and tabulation of results. This makes mail surveys a poor option when dealing with issues such as product development for which prompt decisions are required.

Finally, the accuracy of mail survey results is much more difficult to control than are those obtained through telephone interviews. Respondents often "pick and choose" what they will respond to in a mail survey. Unlike telephone surveys, in which the interviewers can exercise control over skip patterns, mail survey respondents frequently do not follow written instructions carefully.

Steps in Mail Survey Design and Administration

Despite the stated pitfalls, mail surveys often provide an easier solution for small-business owners who have neither the budget nor the staffing to conduct a survey by telephone. Given the frequency of the methodology's use, it is therefore important to discuss the best means of conducting a mail survey. Following are the seven major steps in conducting a mail survey:

1. Develop the questionnaire and cover letter.
2. Obtain survey sample.
3. Print questionnaires and cover letters.
4. Arrange envelopes: outgoing and return postage.
5. Prepare the survey mailing.
6. Code and tabulate survey results.
7. Analyze the results.

Developing the Questionnaire and Cover Letter

Questionnaire development was covered in detail in Chapter 4. However, there are some important differences required in mail surveys that should be discussed here: the need for clear instructions, the deadline and return address, confidentiality, the use of incentives, and the cover letter.

Clear Instructions.

Respondents to mail surveys frequently skim through the questionnaire, choosing which questions to answer. As noted in Chapter 4, it is the researcher's responsibility to make the survey instructions as clear and concise as possible to prevent this from occurring.

When noting instructions for respondents in your mail survey, make them stand out as much as possible; use bold print and capital letters. Leave white space between the instructions and the beginning of the next question to make it easy to read. When you are identifying skip patterns, use arrows to point to the appropriate action given a certain response.

Worksheet 5–1 shows three questions from a survey. How would you correct the questionnaire segment to make it easier for respondents to follow?

Worksheet 5–1

Instructions: Review the following questionnaire and make any changes necessary to simplify it for respondents.

Q15 Did you enjoy your meal at Tony's Restaurant?

    ( ) Yes (Skip to Q17)

    ( ) No (Continue to Q16)

Q16 What was not enjoyable about your meal?

    _____

    _____

Q17 Please rate your overall dining experience during your most recent visit to Tony's Restaurant. [1 = Poor; 5 = Excellent]

        Rating: 1   2   3   4   5

Exhibit 5–1 illustrates how to clarify the questionnaire segment from Worksheet 5–1 to make it easier for potential respondents to understand.

Deadline and Address.

Your questionnaire should also clearly state the survey deadline (usually the last postmarked date from which survey returns will be included in the results), preferably in the introduction paragraph of the questionnaire as well as at the conclusion of the final series of questions. This date should also be in bold print. When the deadline date is shown at the end of the questionnaire, it should be accompanied by the address to which completed surveys should be returned. Even if you provide respondents with return postage-paid envelopes, there is a chance that these will get misplaced.

Exhibit 5–1

Clear Questionnaire Layout

Q15 Did you enjoy your meal at Tony's Restaurant? **[CHECK ONE RESPONSE ONLY]**

    ( ) Yes ——> **[SKIP TO Q17]**

    ( ) No ——> **[CONTINUE TO Q16]**

Q16 What was *not* enjoyable about your meal? **[WRITE YOUR COMMENTS BELOW IN COMPLETE SENTENCES. PLEASE BE SPECIFIC.]**

_____

_____

Q17 Please rate your overall dining experience during your most recent visit to Tony's Restaurant. **[USE A RATING SCALE OF ONE TO FIVE, WHERE 1 = "POOR" AND 5 = "EXCELLENT."]**

    CIRCLE ONE RATING ONLY: 1   2   3   4   5

Providing an address on the questionnaire itself increases the likelihood of survey returns. Exhibit 5–2 provides an example of how deadline dates and return addresses are incorporated at the end of the questionnaire.

Confidentiality.

It is important to avoid asking respondents to provide their names, addresses, or telephone numbers in the questionnaire. By asking for this information, you appear to negate your promise that all results will be kept confidential. This can give respondents a fairly good reason not to return their completed surveys. The only exception to this would be if the information is required to provide the respondents with an incentive for their participation.

Exhibit 5–2

Questionnaire Closing Phrases

Q44 What is your home zip code? _____

Q45 Please indicate your gender:

( ) Female   ( ) Male

This concludes our survey. Thank you for your time and for your opinions. Please mail in your completed questionnaire in the envelope provided no later than **July 16th** so that we will be able to include your responses. If you have misplaced your envelope, questionnaires should be sent to:

Tony's Restaurant
12345 South Palm Boulevard
Tempe, AZ 85282

Exhibit 5–3

Tear-off Section on Survey

Thank you for your time and your opinions. Please return your completed questionnaire in the envelope provided no later than **June 20th** to allow us to include your responses. So that we may send you the gift certificate promised for your time, please complete the following mailing information. This section will be separated from your questionnaire upon receipt so that your responses will remain confidential.

Name: _____

Mailing Address: _____

City: _____ State: _____ Zip Code: _____

In such a case, respondents should be asked to provide such information at the very end of the questionnaire on a tear-off section, which should be separated from the survey immediately upon receipt. Respondents should be assured that this information will be separated from their responses and that they will not be put on any mailing lists.

 The intent of the mail survey is to provide information, not to generate telemarketing or mailing lists.

Incentives.

Although providing **incentives** for returning mail surveys is an accepted practice, it is not always effective or even advisable. Many researchers believe that an offer of cash, product, inclusion in a prize drawing, or other incentive will increase survey response rates. There is most definitely a contingent who will respond to this tactic, but it is usually not large enough to significantly sway the response rate. Those people, particularly among your own customers, who have opinions to voice will do so regardless of any incentive. Consumers who do not like to fill out surveys or believe them to be a waste of time are not necessarily tempted by small tokens. There are, of course, exceptions to every rule—this is based on the author's own experience.

The Cover Letter.

The mail survey's accompanying cover letter is also important to the success of your study. In the cover letter, you should address why you are conducting the survey, stress that the results of the survey will be kept confidential, and identify when and where surveys should be returned. Always thank respondents in advance for their input in the cover letter. A good cover letter can persuade otherwise reluctant persons to respond to your survey.

Even if you are using an outside firm to conduct your mail survey, the cover letter should come from you. A letter from the business owner, president, or (if applicable) the marketing director gives a survey more prestige. It gives potential respondents a feeling of importance and makes them believe that their opinions will affect your operations. Always print the cover letter on your company's letterhead to make it look official and more formal.

Exhibit 5–4

Cover Letter

Dear Valued Customer:

Tony's Restaurant has enjoyed serving you in the past and is now looking toward the future! The enclosed questionnaire will help us evaluate a possible expansion in order to make visiting us even more convenient.

Please take a few minutes and complete this survey. Once you have completed the questionnaire, please return it in the enclosed postage paid envelope no later than June 20th so we can include your responses in our study.

Your opinions are very important to us. Thank you and we look forward to serving you again soon!

Sincerely,

Tony Baker
Proprietor

Obtaining Survey Sample

Survey sampling is the process of identifying the target respondents who can provide the most useful market information, deciding on the number of respondents needed for valid results, allowing for a certain nonresponse rate, and locating a cost-effective list source. (See Chapter 3 for more details.) The principles covered in Chapter 3 also apply to mail survey samples, but the format in which you receive the sample can vary.

When preparing (or ordering) sample for your mail survey, it is best to get two copies of the sample list, one on hard copy and the second on preprinted self-adhesive mailing labels. The hard copy can serve as a backup should the labels get lost in the mailing process or if a second mailing becomes necessary.

Another concern is the format of the sample itself—what to include on the mailing labels. Typically, you will want to include the contact's name (with appropriate title: Mr., Mrs., Miss, Ms., or Dr.) and complete mailing address, including any suite or apartment number and ZIP code. Be sure to check on current postal requirements for bulk mailings to determine other information or preferred ZIP code ordering to speed delivery or cut the costs of your survey mailing.

Also consider how many questionnaires you will need to mail out to ensure that you have the necessary base size of, say, 300 completed surveys returned. Mail surveys typically get returns of about 15 percent. This would mean mailing out approximately 2,000 surveys to guarantee your required return. This assumes that you are mailing to a sample of a large population. If you are mailing to a regular customer base of 500, you would then mail the survey to all of your customers to ensure an adequate number of responses. The response rate might be higher, depending on who is conducting the survey and who the respondents are. Trade associations, credit unions, and nonprofit organizations frequently get higher survey response rates because of the respondents' feelings of affiliation with these organizations.

Printing the Questionnaires and Cover Letters

The questionnaires and cover letters for your mail survey can simply be copied on your office copy machine. Provided that the questionnaire has been created on a computer and looks "camera-ready" and that the printer is not low on toner, this provides an inexpensive alternative to an outside printer. If you cannot spare the copier for a lengthy time period, however, printers will copy these materials for you for a relatively low fee. Do not request typesetting of the questionnaire if it looks good on your original copy. Do, however, consider the size of your questionnaire and the format. Mail surveys can be printed and stapled into booklet format using slightly smaller than average print. Be considerate of your respondents, however; do not make the print too small or they might simply discard the survey.

For cover letters, remember to provide an adequate supply of your letterhead to the printer if they are being copied outside. And do not forget to sign the original letter so that each copy shows a signature. In addition to the questionnaires and the cover letters, bear in mind that you might need to print mailing envelopes (check on the size required based on your questionnaire size) and return envelopes. If you have a return postage permit, be sure to have that information printed on the return envelopes.

Be certain to print about 50 more questionnaires and cover letters than the estimated number needed for your mailing. This provides clean copies if a few are smeared or torn in the mailing process.

Arranging for Envelopes: Outgoing and Return Postage

There are generally two sets of envelopes required for a mail survey: those in which the researcher mails out the survey materials and those in which respondents return their completed surveys. The outgoing envelopes must be labeled with the names and addresses from your sample. When arranging your outgoing mailing, look into bulk rate postage regulations at the post office.

The return envelopes should provide return postage for survey respondents. If you do not have a return postage permit, be sure to put adequate postage on each return envelope. Respondents *might* answer without this courtesy, but you will encourage better response rates with this provision.

Preparing the Survey Mailing

Be certain that each envelope contains a copy of your cover letter, the questionnaire, and the return envelope, as well as any additional materials required for the study. If you are mailing the surveys out first class, check with the post office to confirm any mailing regulations, such as stamping "First Class" on your envelopes. Do not forget to include the amount of time involved in mailing the questionnaires and the time involved in their return by mail when deciding on your survey cutoff date.

Coding and Tabulating Survey Results

As completed questionnaires begin to come in, it is time to begin coding and tabulating the survey results. If at all possible, this is a process that you might prefer to assign to an outside data processing firm. Given a tight budget, however, you can do it internally. It is a simple, albeit very time-consuming, process.

Tabulation basically consists of taking the questions from your survey and setting up some simple grids. Responses run down the left side of your grid and "tick marks" indicate each of the respondents' answers. See Exhibit 5–5 (from question 17 in Exhibit 5–1). When all questions from all of the completed surveys have been tabulated in this manner, these numbers are totaled and percentages are figured. This allows you to determine the opinions and needs of the majority of respondents.

For even greater detail, you can also **cross-tabulate** the survey responses. In other words, you can tabulate responses to questions by the responses given to another selected question, such as age or gender. Headings such as "Gender" are referred to as **banners.** A sample of such a cross-tab table is shown in Exhibit 5–6.

Exhibit 5–5

Tabulation of a Rating Question

Q17 Please rate your overall dining experience during your most recent visit to Tony's Restaurant:

Rating	Number of Responses
1 (Poor)	II
2	III
3	ЖТ II
4	ЖТ ЖТ II
5 (Excellent)	ЖТ III

Exhibit 5–6

Cross-Tabulation of a Rating Question

Q17 Please rate your overall dining experience during your most recent visit to Tony's Restaurant.

	Gender	
Rating	Male	Female
1 (Poor)	I	I
2	II	I
3	III	IIII
4	ЖТ	ЖТ II
5 (Excellent)	III	ЖТ

Again, when all questionnaires have been tallied and percentages figured, you can use this information in your analysis. Provided that bases (number of total respondents) within a cross-tab category are large enough, this type of analysis can provide valuable input from different perspectives. For instance, assume that when all of your tabulations have been completed (see Exhibit 5–6), you find that women are generally rating their dining experience at Tony's Restaurant higher than men responding to the survey. This information would suggest possible actions such as targeting advertising efforts toward women as they appreciate the overall atmosphere or perhaps looking at men's likes and dislikes to better serve this part of your market. In a similar manner, you could determine how different age groups react to the restaurant, how different targets make their restaurant choices, etc.

Frequently, questionnaires include one or more open-ended questions, as discussed in Chapter 4. Compiling these responses requires a process referred to as **coding.** Coding involves reviewing all of the verbatim responses to a given question and grouping like responses. For example, question 16 in Exhibit 5–1 asked survey respondents, "What was *not* enjoyable about your meal?" Assume that responses included the following:

A. "The food was cold."

B. "The waiter was curt and not attentive."

C. "The music was very loud."

D. "The lasagna sat too long before it was served."

E. "My meal wasn't hot when I got it."

Comments A, D and E would be grouped together and assigned a code number with the overall definition: "Food was cold." The responses were not word-for-word the same, but they expressed the same meaning. Such grouping of responses allows verbatim comments to open-ended questions to be tabulated and percentages determined, making analysis easier than if you simply scanned the verbatim responses to look for similarities.

A word of caution is advisable when you are coding survey responses. There are two major mistakes which are made in coding, sometimes even by professionals. First, there is a tendency to try too hard to make comments fit into a specific code. Consider the following comments:

A. "I like the service at Tony's."
B. "I like the food at Tony's."
C. "The food is delicious."
D. "The waitstaff always anticipates my needs."
E. "I like everything about Tony's."

Done correctly, comments B and C would be coded together as "good food"; comments A and D would be coded together as "good service"; and E would be separate. (Obviously, there would be far more comments than this to be coded.) A common mistake would be, for example, to group A, B and E together as "like restaurant overall." You must pay careful attention to what is being said and make certain that the comments fit well into the specified code. Think of this as a jigsaw puzzle, a piece either fits or it does not, you cannot force it and have the puzzle look right in the end. Another error that occurs is just the opposite; rather than making an effort to have only a few codes, the person coding is over cautious and assigns separate codes to everything. This defeats the purpose of coding altogether. For instance, in the preceding example, comments B and C would receive separate codes because comment B did not say specifically that it is the taste of the food he or she likes.

Analyzing the Survey Results

Quantitative studies are much more clear-cut to analyze than are qualitative studies. By looking at the responses to each question as well as your cross-tabulated figures, you can determine the needs and interests of the majority of respondents based on the percentages you have compiled. If only 6 percent heard about Tony's Restaurant on the radio, but 31 percent saw the newspaper advertisement, then the current radio advertising is not as effective as print media for reaching the target market. This does not say *why* it is not as effective; to find that out would require another question. This does, however, provide input for Tony's advertising decisions.

Two issues require consideration when you are conducting your analysis. First, if the respondent base for any given question or cross-tab category is notably small (say, under 50 when you have 300 returns), avoid detailed analysis of that item. The results might not be an accurate reflection of the market as a whole. Second, avoid drawing final conclusions when the precise question has not been asked. As noted above, you might recognize that the radio ads are not effective, but this does not tell you whether advertising on another station, using a different radio ad, or changing your time slots would prove to be an effective alternative.

 A survey can only provide answers when the questions are asked.

Terms to Remember

Banner Headings used in data tables of survey results

Coding The process of reviewing all of the verbatim responses to a given question and grouping like responses for analysis

Cross-tabulate To tabulate responses to survey questions by the responses given to another selected question such as age, gender, or income level

Incentive A form of compensation provided if a person responds as requested to a survey or otherwise participates in a research study

Chapter Six

Developing a Winning Telephone Survey

Drawbacks and Benefits of Telephone Surveys

From a small-business standpoint, telephone surveys are more difficult to conduct in-house than are mail surveys. In fact, unless you have access to several people who can spend several hours on the phone for about a week, using an outside vendor to conduct the telephone interviewing will probably be necessary.

Although the expenses related to telephone surveys can be a drawback, there are definite advantages to using this methodology. The results from telephone surveys are available much more quickly than are mail survey responses—often within three weeks. There is also greater potential for quality control. Interviewers are trained to know the questionnaire and its skip patterns. Respondents will therefore answer all of the correct questions (unless they refuse to answer a question), unlike mail surveys, in which responses can sometimes appear haphazard.

Steps in Conducting a Telephone Survey

The following seven basic guidelines are useful when conducting a telephone survey:

1. Develop the questionnaire.
2. Obtain survey sample.
3. Brief the interviewers.
4. Conduct a survey pretest.
5. Collect the data.
6. Code and tabulate the survey results.
7. Analyze the results.

Developing the Questionnaire

Questionnaire development for telephone surveys follows the steps identified in Chapter 4. For a telephone survey, however, the instructions you provide with each question are for the interviewer, rather than for the respondent as in mail surveys. Consider Exhibit 4–3, repeated now in Worksheet 6–1. How would you revise this segment of a mail questionnaire for a telephone survey? The corrected version is presented in Exhibit 6–1. Notice in particular the use of capital letters to designate items that are *not* to be read aloud to respondents.

Worksheet 6–1

Instructions: Revise the following questionnaire segment for use in a telephone survey.

Tony's Restaurant
Customer Survey

Date: _____ / _____ / _____

Tony's Restaurant is considering opening a second location. To identify the site that would best serve our clientele, we are conducting a brief survey of our customers. Please take a few minutes to answer this questionnaire. All of your responses will be kept confidential. When you turn in your completed questionnaire, our cashier will provide you with a 2-for-1 coupon for your next visit. Thank you!

Q1 Approximately how many times have you dined at Tony's during the past 12 months? [CHECK ONE RESPONSE ONLY BELOW]

( ) This is the first time ——> [CONTINUE TO Q2]

( ) 2–5 times ——> [SKIP TO Q3]

( ) 6–10 times ——> [SKIP TO Q3]

( ) 11 times or more ——> [SKIP TO Q3]

Q2 [ANSWER ONLY IF THIS IS YOUR FIRST VISIT]

How did you first hear about Tony's? [CHECK ONE RESPONSE ONLY]

( ) Newspaper ad

( ) Radio ad

( ) Friend/family member/business associate recommended it

( ) Received coupon in the mail

( ) Drove by and saw it

( ) Other [SPECIFY: _____]

( ) Do not recall

——> [SKIP TO Q4] <——

(Continued)

Q3 What is the *main* reason you choose to dine at Tony's? [CHECK ONE REASON ONLY BELOW]

( ) Reasonable prices

( ) Good food

( ) Friendly staff

( ) Menu selection

( ) Close to home

( ) Close to work

( ) Coupons are available

( ) My friends/family like to eat here

( ) Other [SPECIFY: _____]

Q4 Do you *usually* (or, if this is your first time, did you) come to Tony's from home or from work? [CHECK ONE ONLY BELOW]

( ) Home

( ) Work

( ) Other [SPECIFY: _____]

Q5 And how far do you typically travel to get to Tony's? [CHECK ONE ONLY BELOW]

( ) Less than one mile

( ) 1–2 miles

( ) 3–4 miles

( ) 5–10 miles

( ) 11–20 miles

( ) Over 20 miles

(Continued)

Worksheet 6-1

Q6 On a rating scale of one to five, where one means "not at all important" and five means "very important," please rate how important each of the following aspects are to you personally when selecting a restaurant.
[CIRCLE ONE RESPONSE PER ITEM]

	Not at all Important				Very Important
a. Atmosphere	1	2	3	4	5
b. Price	1	2	3	4	5
c. Location	1	2	3	4	5
d. Good food	1	2	3	4	5
e. Menu selection	1	2	3	4	5
f. Service	1	2	3	4	5

Exhibit 6–1

Revised Telephone Survey Script: Tony's Restaurant Customer Survey

Interviewer: _____ **Date:** ___ / ___ / ___

Hello, my name is _____, calling on behalf of Tony's Restaurant. Tony's is considering opening a second location. To identify the site that would best serve our clientele, we are conducting a brief survey of our customers. This will only take a few minutes, and all of your responses will be kept confidential.

Q1 Approximately how many times have you dined at Tony's during the past 12 months? [DO NOT READ LIST. CHECK ONE RESPONSE ONLY BELOW]

( ) THIS IS THE FIRST TIME ——> [CONTINUE TO Q2]

( ) 2–5 TIMES ——> [SKIP TO Q3]

( ) 6–10 TIMES ——> [SKIP TO Q3]

( ) 11 TIMES OR MORE ——> [SKIP TO Q3]

( ) DO NOT KNOW

( ) REFUSED

Q2 [ASK ONLY IF RESPONDENT SAID THIS WAS FIRST VISIT]

How did you first hear about Tony's? [DO NOT READ LIST. CHECK ONE RESPONSE ONLY]

( ) NEWSPAPER AD

( ) RADIO AD

( ) FRIEND/FAMILY MEMBER/BUSINESS ASSOCIATE RECOMMENDED IT

( ) RECEIVED COUPON IN THE MAIL

( ) DROVE BY AND SAW IT

( ) OTHER [SPECIFY: _____]

( ) DO NOT RECALL

( ) NO RESPONSE

——> [SKIP TO Q4] <——

(Continued)

Exhibit 6–1 (Continued)

Q3 What is the *main* reason you choose to dine at Tony's? [DO NOT READ LIST. CHECK ONE ONLY BELOW]

( ) REASONABLE PRICES

( ) GOOD FOOD

( ) FRIENDLY STAFF

( ) MENU SELECTION

( ) CLOSE TO HOME

( ) CLOSE TO WORK

( ) COUPONS ARE AVAILABLE

( ) MY FRIENDS/FAMILY LIKE TO EAT HERE

( ) OTHER [SPECIFY:_____]

( ) NO PARTICULAR REASON

( ) NO RESPONSE

Q4 Do you usually (OR, IF THIS IS FIRST TIME: "Did you . . .") come to Tony's from home or from work? [DO NOT READ LIST. CHECK ONE ONLY BELOW]

( ) HOME

( ) WORK

( ) OTHER [SPECIFY:_____]

( ) NO RESPONSE

Q5 And how far do you typically travel to get to Tony's? Would you say . . . [READ LIST AND CHECK FIRST RESPONSE ONLY]

( ) Less than one mile,

( ) 1–2 miles,

( ) 3–4 miles,

( ) 5–10 miles,

( ) 11–20 miles, or

( ) Over 20 miles?

(Continued)

Exhibit 6–1

( ) (DO NOT READ) DO NOT KNOW

( ) (DO NOT READ) REFUSED

Q6 On a rating scale of one to five, where one means "not at all important" and five means "very important," please rate how important each of the following aspects are to you personally when selecting a restaurant. [READ EACH ITEM AND CIRCLE ONE RATING PER ITEM. REPEAT SCALE AS NEEDED FOR RESPONDENT]

	Not at all Important			Very Important		No Response
a. Atmosphere	1	2	3	4	5	6
b. Price	1	2	3	4	5	6
c. Location	1	2	3	4	5	6
d. Good food	1	2	3	4	5	6
e. Menu selection	1	2	3	4	5	6
f. Service	1	2	3	4	5	6

What differences did you notice between the telephone and mail versions of the questionnaire? Following are the main points that differ based on this particular example:

- All items that are not to be read aloud to respondents appear in capital letters in the telephone version.

- Instructions are now targeted at interviewers rather than respondents.

- "Do not know" and "No response" categories are added to most questions to allow for these possible results (although interviewers should attempt to get actual responses).

The survey introduction plays an important role in convincing people to participate in your survey. With rampant phone fraud, it is important to put respondents at ease immediately. Clearly identify who is calling and what the survey is being used for. Stress that responses will be kept confidential. It is also a common practice to mention in the introduction that the interviewer will not be attempting to sell respondents anything.

Instructions in the body of the questionnaire are essential even if professional interviewers will be conducting the survey. Research vendors generally use some form of computer-aided telephone interviewing (CATI) system to conduct interviews. Questionnaires are preprogrammed so that skip patterns are automatically handled for the interview based on the responses entered. These instructions help the programmer to set the survey up correctly. For your own interviewers, the instructions will help to ensure consistency in how questions are asked and how responses are recorded.

At the end of your survey, interviewers can identify whether the respondent is male or female. Do *not* ask this as a demographic question on a telephone survey. (You might laugh, but it has been known to happen!) Interviewers should also confirm the phone number they dialed before concluding an interview: "And may I confirm that I reached you at . . .?" This allows for call validation (discussed in Chapter 9). Finally, at the end of the questionnaire, add a brief script calling for interviewers to thank respondents for their time and input.

Obtaining Survey Sample

Effective survey sampling requires the researcher to identify appropriate target respondents, decide on a valid sample size, allow for a certain nonresponse rate, and locate cost-effective list sources. (See Chapter 3.)

For telephone surveys, it is crucial that the sample provides telephone numbers including *area codes* for each person or company listed. If you are ordering lists from a list broker, be certain that you provide all of the necessary specifications. If you have **quotas** (required segments to be contacted, such as X interviews in one ZIP code and X in another), request separate lists for each, if possible, or at least a definite break in the list between groupings.

Briefing Interviewers

Even professional research vendors require interviewer **briefings** before starting new telephone surveys. Read the entire questionnaire aloud with the interviewers. Allow them to ask questions about the wording, your instructions, etc. You want to be sure that they are comfortable with the questionnaire and understand it thoroughly. Role-playing often helps to familiarize interviewers with a questionnaire. To do this, you would assign one interviewer to act as the respondent while another practices conducting the interview.

In the briefing session, stress the importance of reading the questions precisely as they are worded to keep the survey consistent. Also explain **probing** and **clarification** techniques to your interviewers.

Probing involves encouraging respondents to elaborate on their responses. For example, assume that you have asked a respondent where he or she saw or heard your advertising in the past three weeks. The respondent says, "In the newspaper." To probe for additional responses, you might say, "Where else have you seen the ads in the past three weeks?" He or she might add, "On TV," to which you could respond, "Anywhere else?"

Probing questions are used to encourage additional responses. You should not ask, "Did you see the TV ad?" or other leading questions to probe respondents. Also, interviewers should not probe respondents if an instruction says to "record only one response." Probing is, however, common when asking open-ended questions or questions requiring a list of responses. The best way to ensure the proper use of probing is to identify in your instructions whether probing is recommended.

Clarification of responses is a technique used by interviewers to make sure they have understood each answer. If you ask a respondent where he or she received information on recycling, and she says the D.O.E., the interviewer should clarify the meaning of the acronym, *even if he or she is quite sure what it means.* The interviewer might clarify the term by saying, "Could you define that for me?" or "What do you mean by . . .?" in order to obtain the complete response, "the Department of Energy." Clarification is also used for getting definitions of foreign phrases, slang, or technical terms with which the interviewer is not familiar or that are not commonly used.

Conducting a Survey Pretest

The survey **pretest** is conducted to test the length of the interviews and the **incidence rate** of respondents as well as respondents' comprehension of the questionnaire. Generally, 10–20 interviews are conducted immediately following a briefing. "Red flags" that can signify the need for questionnaire revisions are explained in Exhibit 6–2. A survey pretest can identify problems including overly long surveys, confusing wording, complicated question formats, and unrealistic respondent qualifications. Discovering such problems early allows changes to be made that will prevent unnecessary hours of unproductive interviewing.

Exhibit 6–2

Warning Signs in Telephone Survey Pretests

"Red Flag"	Potential Problem
1. Interviews last over 12 minutes	Unless the survey is about an extremely interesting subject or current issue, long interviews are likely to discourage respondents from completing the survey.
2. Respondents answer questions with questions	If respondents do not understand what you are asking, they will probably ask what you mean, why you want to know, etc. This will slow the survey down.
3. Long pauses before respondents answer certain questions	If a question is complicated, such as ranking ten items, it will confuse respondents, slow down the survey, and produce uncertain results.
4. Low incidence of qualified respondents	If you are experiencing difficulties finding respondents, perhaps your qualifications are not realistic or you will need additional sample and more interviewing time.

Collecting Data

When the pretest has been completed and all resulting survey revisions have been made, data collection can begin. How long interviewing will take depends on many factors, including the interviewer's skills, length of the interviews, the number of completed surveys required, established quotas, and so on. At the end of each "shift," you should tally the number of complete questionnaires, paying special attention to any quota requirements. **Editing** should be an ongoing process. (See Chapter 9.) Carefully review questionnaires to ensure that responses are being marked properly and that skip patterns are being followed.

Coding and Tabulating Survey Results

If you have conducted your own survey on paper using staff or others as interviewers, then the coding and tabulation process for the telephone survey will mirror the process explained in Chapter 5. If your survey has been conducted using a research vendor, they will typically provide you with these services as part of their survey estimate.

Analyzing the Results

Telephone surveys like mail surveys, described in Chapter 5, also produce quantitative results. The same techniques described in Chapter 5 should be considered when you are analyzing the results of your telephone survey.

Ethical Considerations in Telephone Surveys

When you are conducting a telephone survey, you should never utilize the phone number provided in the sample to call a participant back for any reason other than to validate data. There should be no attempt to invade a person's privacy. If a potential respondent is contacted and declines to participate in your survey or refuses to answer particular questions, this reaction should be respected. Never harass or complain to a contact.

In all surveys and focus groups, the confidentiality of results is stressed. Never identify a respondent by name in a report or evaluation, particularly when you are discussing particular comments that person has made. Never release sensitive or personal information such as age, income, telephone numbers, etc., to any other person or company. This means that you should not sell your lists or any information that specifies who your respondents were by name or other identifying factor.

Terms to Remember

Briefing An interviewer training session specifically related to a new survey or study

Clarification Asking respondents to further define their responses, such as stating a complete name versus an acronym

Editing A careful review of completed questionnaires to ensure that all skip patterns and indicated instructions have been followed correctly

Incidence rate The percentage of qualified respondents within a given population

Pretest A "trial run," usually of a telephone survey, consisting of approximately 10–20 interviews to test the length of the survey, question wording, etc.

Probing Process by which interviewers encourage survey respondents to elaborate on their responses

Quotas Preassigned segments of survey sample to be interviewed, such as 50 percent females and 50 percent males

Chapter Seven

Focus Groups

To the uninitiated, focus groups are appealing because they appear as simple to arrange as any casual conversation. However, focus groups require careful planning and coordination, at least one month's time. Two or more focus groups are generally conducted to provide adequate input and to allow for comparisons between groups (e.g., how customers' attitudes compare to those of noncustomers).

Developing a Focus Group Study Topic

First you need to ensure that the topic you want to study actually lends itself to a focus group methodology. If you are looking for numbers to validate a decision, this is not the way to go. If, however, you want to present advertising concepts, show visuals, discuss policies, or develop new names or products, focus groups provide an excellent forum.

What is your main topic, the one you will *focus* on in the group(s)? To practice developing a topic, we will continue to use the example of Tony's Restaurant from earlier chapters. The restaurant owner wants to change the "look" of the establishment's menus. Exhibit 7–1 shows the image that is currently on the cover of the menu.

Tony has lately become concerned that this cover does not portray the right image for his restaurant. He thinks that it gives the impression that it has a "party" atmosphere, rather than the intimate dining atmosphere he wishes to portray. He has a few ideas in mind to replace the current image. (See Exhibit 7–2.) Armed with these options, the business owner decides to conduct some focus groups to determine which cover would have the most positive effect on sales. Given his budget limitations, Tony decides to do the research himself.

Exhibit 7–1

Existing Menu Cover Image

Exhibit 7–2

Possible Replacement Menu Cover Images

Steps in Conducting a Focus Group

Tony is aware of the need to plan carefully to organize and successfully conduct a focus group study. He will follow 14 basic steps:

1. Determine the study objectives.
2. Determine participant profile(s) and number of groups.
3. Develop focus groups screener questionnaires.
4. Develop a moderator's discussion guide.
5. Arrange to videotape and/or audiotape focus group sessions.
6. Arrange for a place to hold the group(s).
7. Recruit participants.
8. Send confirmation letters and directions to participants.
9. Arrange for refreshments (if applicable).
10. Get co-op fees.
11. Prepare for focus group session(s) at site.
12. Moderate the focus group(s).
13. Pay participants co-op fees.
14. Analyze the results of focus group(s).

Developing Focus Group Study Objectives

Tony has already chosen his main goal for this study: to find the best cover image for his restaurant's menu. Using the procedure described in Chapter 1, he expands his objectives by developing a "wish list." As a result, he has decided on several objectives for the study:

- Identifying his establishment's current image among both customers and noncustomers
- Determining what most encourages repeat business (price, location, selection, image, quality, service, etc.)
- Obtaining feedback on his current menu, specifically the cover
- Testing proposed menu covers

Focus groups are not quantitative; therefore, your objectives cannot include numerical goals such as, "Developing sales projections based on customers' reactions to various menu covers."

Determining the Participant Profile and Number of Groups

After objectives have been set, Tony needs to decide what group of people will best provide him with the input he needs as well as how many groups he will conduct. First he addresses the participant issue. He obviously wants to talk with current customers who are familiar with his establishment. He decides that noncustomers could also provide a different perspective, particularly in determining what image would help attract new customers to the restaurant. He also considers a third type of participant—persons who have visited once in the past year, but who have not been back since. He ultimately rejects this profile because it would be difficult and expensive to identify these particular people.

Tony is certain that he can identify the customer group based on his own "preferred guest" records. He maintains this database to assist his waitstaff in better serving his frequent visitors. He plans to contact noncustomers via telephone calls to residents of the three-ZIP-code area surrounding the restaurant. He will purchase this list from a telephone service provider.

Price is a major consideration for Tony when determining how many focus groups he will conduct. Given that he has only one location, he chooses to hold just two focus groups:

- One of current customers—to be defined as having dined at his restaurant at least three times in the past six months
- One of noncustomers—to be defined as those who have not dined at the restaurant within the past two years

Developing Focus Group Screener Questionnaires

Once Tony has established whom to **recruit** for his groups, as well as the number of groups that he plans to conduct, he is ready to draft the **screener questionnaires.** These brief questionnaires will be used to **qualify** potential participants for both groups by ensuring that they meet the criteria of the profile that has been selected.

For example, Tony wants to make sure that his customer group consists only of people who have eaten at his restaurant at least three times in the past six months. His noncustomer group should consist only of persons who dine out at least once a month, but not at his restaurant within the past year or more. He also needs to avoid inviting competitors' employees to attend the groups, so an appropriate question should be added to screen these individuals out of the group. (See question 3 in Exhibit 7–3.)

Exhibit 7–3 shows the screener for the proposed customer group. The screener should take only about five minutes to complete on the phone. Remember, however, that not every person that Tony or his staff contacts will be qualified or able to attend. This means that many more calls will be made than just the exact number of people required for the focus group(s).

When looking at the screener, one of the first things a nonresearcher generally comments on is the phrase, "Thank respondent and terminate." It might sound like the interviewer is given permission to "deal with" nonresponsive or nonqualified respondents, but this simply means, "End the call." (Consider this the author's disclaimer should you become frustrated with various respondents!)

Developing the Moderator's Discussion Guide

Developing the **moderator's discussion guide** for focus groups can be done at any point before the day of the first focus group. For the novice, however, it is highly recommended that you complete this task early on in the process to allow adequate time for revisions and moderating practice, if necessary. The guide is basically an outline to assist the moderator in conducting the group(s) in an orderly manner and to ensure that all necessary topics are touched on during the course of the group(s).

Exhibit 7-3

Customer Group Screener: Tony's Restaurant Menu Focus Groups

DATE: ___ /___ /___ CONTACT NAME: _____

PHONE NUMBER DIALED: (_____) _____ – _____

RECRUITER: _____

Hello, my name is _____, calling for Tony's Restaurant in Anytown. May I please speak with [NAME OF CUSTOMER FROM LIST]? [IF CORRECT PERSON, CONTINUE; IF NOT, HOLD AND REPEAT GREETING; IF NOT AVAILABLE, SCHEDULE CALLBACK TIME]

We are conducting a research study to help us in making some important marketing decisions, and we would like to include your opinions.

Q1 First, can you tell me if during the past six months you have dined at Tony's *at least* three times?

( ) Yes ——————> [CONTINUE TO Q2]

( ) No

( ) Do not know ——> [THANK RESPONDENTS & TERMINATE

( ) Refused

Q2 And are you 18 years of age or older?

( ) Yes ——————> [CONTINUE TO Q3]

( ) No ——————> [THANK RESPONDENT & TERMINATE]

( ) Refused

Q3 Are you currently employed by a restaurant or other food service provider?

( ) Yes ——————> [THANK RESPONDENT & TERMINATE]

( ) No ——————> [CONTINUE TO Q4]

( ) Refused ——————> [THANK RESPONDENT & TERMINATE]

(Continued)

Exhibit 7–3

Q4 We will be conducting a focus group discussion on Wednesday night, January 15th, at 7:30 P.M., in the banquet room at Tony's Restaurant. You will be served refreshments and compensated $25 for your participation. Will you be able to join us at that time?

( ) Yes ——————> [PROVIDE DIRECTIONS & GET COMPLETE NAME & MAILING ADDRESS TO SEND CONFIRMATION]

( ) No ——————> [THANK RESPONDENT & TERMINATE]

Contact's Name: _____

Mailing Address: _____

City/State: _____ **ZIP code:** _____

The best starting point for the development of the discussion guide is the objectives you have set for the study. Look back for a moment to Tony's market research objectives for his proposed groups. Using these, try to develop a *brief* outline of potential issues for participants to discuss. Each objective should serve as a major outline bullet point, as shown in Worksheet 7–1.

Worksheet 7–1

Instructions: Develop an outline of potential issues to discuss in Tony's Restaurant customer focus group.

- **Identifying establishment's current image (among customers)**
  - _____
  - _____
  - _____

- **Determining what most encourages repeat business**
  - _____
  - _____
  - _____

- **Obtaining feedback on current menu (specifically the cover)**
  - _____
  - _____
  - _____

- **Testing proposed menu covers**
  - _____
  - _____
  - _____

Focus group moderators have varying styles, both in their discussion guides and in the way that they conduct groups. For the moment, we are concentrating on the discussion guide itself. At a later point, we will deal with moderating styles and how to maintain control of the discussion. The best moderator's guide is whatever works best for *you*. You can format the bullet points as questions or simply list brief topics to remind you about what to cover in the group(s). It is important that you be comfortable enough with the structure that you can look up from the outline to speak without getting confused. Exhibit 7–4 is one potential version of a moderator's discussion guide for Tony's menu focus groups with customers.

Arranging to Videotape and/or Audiotape Group Sessions

Arranging to record the focus groups on audiotape or videotape is by far the simplest of the steps involved with planning focus groups. Videotaping of focus groups is preferable, because it allows you not only to see hands raised in response to questions, but also to note any pertinent body language that occurs during the discussion. If your budget does not allow for a professional service to tape the group(s) for you, a home video camera will suffice. It is highly recommended, however, that you place someone else in charge of the taping to free you from checking on the tape throughout the group. In addition, it is important that the person assigned to the task of videotaping be familiar with the camera being used. It is not uncommon to experience group tapes with no video and/or no audio because the videotape "coordinator" had never used the equipment before the focus group.

Audiotaping of focus groups should *always* be conducted. This provides backup just in case the videotaping fails. It also is an alternative to videotaping. On a small budget, audiotaping will provide you with workable input for reporting, although it is harder to follow when you cannot see the speakers and the related nods, expressions, and gestures. Again, however, it is important to provide backup taping. If you are working solely with audiotaping, be sure to do so with two separate recorders to cover you should one recorder fail to pick up the audio properly.

Focus group participants should be advised that their sessions are being audiotaped and/or videotaped. Participants should also be told if anyone not visible to them is viewing the groups. It is not necessary to identify precisely who the viewers are, but do mention that your "associates" or "assistants" are viewing the groups.

Exhibit 7–4

Customer Discussion Guide: Tony's Restaurant Menu Focus Groups

(10 min.)   INTRODUCTION
- Greeting
- Purpose of focus group: opportunity to discuss/offer opinions about restaurant marketing/menus
- Ground rules:
  - Role of moderator
  - Recording equipment/viewers (if applicable)
  - Confidentiality of comments (no "right" or "wrong" answers)
  - Speak one at a time/as clearly as possible
  - Brief "get-acquainted" period: Names/favorite cuisine

(20 min.)   RESTAURANT PATRONAGE
- At which restaurants do you dine at least once a month? Two or more times per month?
  - For what meals?
  - Why do you specifically choose these restaurants? [Referrals, convenience, price, menu selection, etc.]
- How often do you dine at Tony's? Generally for what meals?
- Why do you select Tony's?

(20 min.)   RESTAURANT IMAGE
- Do you connect certain images with different restaurants? [Examples]
- If so, explain how you derive these images. [Elite because of price, trendy because of decor, etc.]
- When you think of [select two restaurants mentioned in Patronage section plus Tony's]:
  - What words best describe each of these restaurants? Why?
  - What role do the following play in creating their image:
    Price? Decor? Menus? Clientele?

(10 min.)   BREAK

(Continued)

Exhibit 7–4

(20 min.) MENU COVERS
- Show menu samples.
  - What type of image do these menu covers convey? Why?
  - Which do you prefer? Why?
- Indicate current cover versus new options.
  - Which recommended? Why?
  - What type of selection do you expect with each of these covers? Why?

(10 min.) CONCLUSION/FINAL COMMENTS

Arranging for a Place to Hold the Groups

In the example of Tony's Restaurant, the groups (per the screener questionnaire) are to be held in the restaurant's banquet room. Wherever the groups are held, you need to allow comfortable spacing between participants. It is preferable for seating to be in a circle. A conference table is typically used for group seating. However, seating in a "living room" setting in which participants are seated in a circular pattern would be just as workable.

In the best-case scenario, focus groups are held at a professional market research facility in a **focus group room.** These rooms are set up as a large conference room with a conference table seating 8–13 persons comfortably with the moderator seated at one end. At the opposite end of the room is a one-way mirror, behind which are usually seated several client representatives. These clients are able to hear and view the groups without being seen by the group participants. Frequently, the videotaping equipment is also mounted in the viewing room behind the mirror to prevent distracting participants.

Although this is a wonderful set-up, it is not necessarily feasible for a smaller business with a limited focus group budget. Other options need to be considered, as Tony did when choosing to use his banquet room. His participants are aware that he is sponsoring the study, so there is really no reason not to hold the groups on site at the restaurant.

Suppose, however, that you want to conduct groups to identify customer service trends in your industry and you do *not* want participants to know that your company is conducting the groups. Assuming that you have a small budget, where else could you conduct the groups? One solution that works very well is to use a hotel meeting room at a centralized location. These rooms are generally reasonably priced and can be set up to accommodate however many participants you are expecting. One drawback is that you frequently are expected to use the hotel's food service if you require refreshments for your participants. This, however, is usually offset by the cost savings incurred by using the hotel's meeting room versus a market research facility. Other options for places to hold the groups include library meeting rooms, college or school facilities, or area restaurants, all of which are usually available for a minimal charge, if not free.

Recruiting Participants

Once you have determined whom you will include in your focus group(s) as well as when and where they will actually be conducted, you are ready to begin the recruiting process. When conducted by professionals, the recruiting process is typically done through telephone calls to potential participants using a screener. (See Exhibit 7–3.)

Depending on the participant qualifications, it could take up to 10 or more calls to recruit a single person for a group. Eight to ten recruits are considered a good working group. There are enough participants to get strong input, but not so many that the group gets out of control and confused. To guarantee that 8–10 participants actually will show up for your groups, it is generally recommended that you recruit between 12 and 14 persons.

Bear in mind that it is uncommon for all 14 people who agreed to attend to show up for a given group. Invariably, there will be a person who forgets, another who is ill, and the occasional person who regrets committing himself or herself for the focus group when a better offer comes along.

In Tony's case, he has limited time and staff resources to conduct the study in this manner. He decides to try two different means of recruiting to ease the amount of telephone time required. He will recruit the noncustomer group by telephone using the list he purchased earlier. He develops a screener that qualifies participants by confirming that they have not dined at his establishment within the past two years, but that they do dine out frequently and do reside within the three-ZIP-code area. In order to randomize the list, he plans to contact every fifth name on the list. He has asked waitstaff/host staff who are not scheduled during given evening shifts over a four-night period to assist in the recruiting effort. Given the limited phone capacity for this type of activity and his confidence in these particular employees, they have all agreed that it would be easiest if they each took a portion of the randomized list and placed the recruiting calls from their homes. In return for their calling efforts, each participating staff person will receive a bonus check.

For the current customer group, Tony has decided to do a mailing to his "preferred guest list" inviting interested persons to call and request a screening. The group will be filled on a "first qualified, first invited" basis, with callers being screened by any available staff member using the previously developed screener. Note that given this change in the recruiting process, the introduction section of the screener would require some minor modifications. Although this is less "scientific" than random calling from a list as in the noncustomer version, it cuts down Tony's staff's hours on the phone and should help to speed up the recruiting process. Remember that focus groups provide qualitative, subjective results. Because they are not projectable to a larger population, this type of sampling should not pose any threat to the integrity of the study. In addition, Tony is concerned that calling his regular customers could appear somewhat invasive. This method solves this problem for him.

Sending Confirmation Letters to Recruits

Assume now that after significant effort all participants have been successfully recruited for Tony's focus groups. Approximately 5–7 days before the scheduled groups, he will send out **confirmation letters** to all scheduled participants for each group. This letter will include a brief thank-you to recruits for agreeing to participate, directions (preferably in map form) to the location where the group is scheduled, and a reminder about the time and date for which the group is scheduled. It is advisable to ask participants to plan on arriving about ten minutes early so that the group will be able to start on time. In addition, confirm what co-op payment the participants will be receiving—this is your last chance to reinforce their interest in attending!

Often focus group participants are new to this research procedure. Many show up for groups with children in tow, spouses who came along for the ride, or a friend who heard about the group and wants to make a "quick $25." It obviously is not practical (nor is it good research) to include these additional people. In the case of children, your firm becomes liable for them while they are on-site. If proper supervision is not available, you risk liability problems. Therefore, you should also include a brief explanation in your confirmation letters to recruits that addresses precisely these problems. Explain that they are not to bring children along because there are no means of properly accommodating them. Drivers, spouses, and friends are welcome to wait for them in the lobby (or, in Tony's case, perhaps profitably in the lounge!), but given the research nature of the study they will not be able to join recruits in the group itself. By remembering to add these simple items in the confirmation letter, you will avoid confusion and ill feelings at the time of your focus groups.

Finally, the confirmation letter should also encourage recruits to call a specific contact if for some reason they become unable to attend. Be sure that both a contact name and telephone number are provided for this purpose. This allows time to recruit additional participants if calls are received soon enough. At the very least, changes can be made to seating and refreshment orders.

Arranging for Refreshments

This particular step is actually done more in conjunction with arranging for a facility for your focus groups. It is, however, not until you have a more precise count of how many participants to expect that you can properly finalize this aspect of your focus group arrangements.

Focus group refreshments are best kept light and easy to eat. Usually, when groups are held in the evening, the initial group (say, about 6:00 P.M.) is served a light delicatessen-style selection: finger sandwiches, fresh fruit and vegetable trays, and a selection of beverages and coffee. A later group, around 8:00 P.M., would simply be served a cookie or other dessert tray, also accompanied by a beverage selection and coffee. If the refreshments served are too heavy or messy, you risk having a tired or preoccupied group; it becomes an eating event rather than a discussion. Although Tony operates a restaurant, his selection offers little that is appropriate focus group fare. He arranges for a local deli to make up trays of sandwiches and desserts to be used in the groups. His restaurant will provide the necessary beverage service.

Getting Co-Op Fees

This item might not really seem worthy of a separate discussion, but it would look very bad for Tony if he completed his groups and then realized he had forgotten to get the money to pay the participants.

As a general practice, participants are paid the **co-op fees** in cash unless some other form of co-op has been selected, such as gift certificates or merchandise. Nonprofit organizations typically offer a small "promo" item in lieu of cash, whereas many companies offer products or gifts based on their own business. If people are willing to attend based on noncash incentives, these can encourage repeat business at an establishment.

 Consumers are becoming increasingly "marketing savvy." They are often familiar with focus groups and co-op procedures; cash is often expected!

If you are paying your participants in cash, be certain that the amount you get from the bank is in the proper denominations to correctly divide up the amount by participant. Usually co-op fees are put in separate envelopes for each participant to simplify "doling out" these funds at the completion of a focus group.

Preparing for Focus Group Session(s) at the Site

You now have recruited your focus groups, confirmed attendance by your letter, and made all necessary arrangements for the facility and refreshments. Your moderator's discussion guide is ready, and you have all of the co-op fees neatly sorted out into envelopes. So what's left? Now comes the toughest part! It is time to actually conduct the focus groups.

First, remember to arrive at your selected location well in advance of your participants. You need to have control of the groups from the start. Set up and test all of your audiovisual equipment before the arrival of your first participants. Be sure that all sound and video are recording properly and that participants will be heard from all angles in the room. If you are doing the taping yourself, one means of ensuring that everyone gets picked up on tape is to place your video equipment at the head of the room (near where you plan to be seated) and the tape recorder(s) at the opposite end or along the sides of the room, depending on the available space.

Once the equipment is tested and refreshments are set up, you will want to review your discussion guide once more before the groups start. It is hardly expected that even a seasoned research professional will have memorized the discussion guide, but you should be comfortable with the general direction the discussion is expected to take. Above all, particularly if you do not frequently speak to groups of people, remember that your role is simply to facilitate the discussion. You will ask questions to get the conversation flowing and occasionally will redirect participants to a specific topic. You are not on stage in the group—the participants are. This should alleviate any premoderating jitters.

Moderating the Focus Group(s)

The discussion guide alone does not ensure that the participants will cover all of the issues in the usual 90-minute focus group. It is the moderator's task to keep the group "on task" by encouraging all participants to offer their opinions, preventing overly opinionated people from dominating the others, and preventing any biases from invading the group. At this time, we will cover some basic instructions and techniques to assist you in moderating your own focus groups.

First, reiterate to participants the information they initially heard when they were being recruited: what a focus group is (in general terms) and what the main purpose of this particular focus group is. Advise them that no response or comment is considered "right" or "wrong," and that everyone's opinion is important to this research study. Do not forget to remind them to speak one at a time and in clear, perhaps slightly louder than usual voices to ensure that their comments are picked up on the tapes.

You should definitely point out the recording equipment to participants to be sure that they are aware that they will be taped during the session. It is rare for a participant to refuse to stay in a group because of the taping process. Simply explain that you need these tapes as records to use in your analysis and that individuals will never be identified by name in the focus group report. Most participants accept this without question and, in fact, once the group gets involved in the subject at hand, most appear to forget the taping equipment altogether.

Even though you are aware of your role in the group, do not assume that the group participants are. Explain that you are there to make sure that all necessary aspects of the study get touched on to some degree. Tell them that you will be trying to make sure everyone gets a chance to voice their opinions, but, in order to do so, you might occasionally have to cut another participant off at a certain point. Assure them that they should not take this personally; you simply need to cover a great amount of material in a limited amount of time.

Also discourage side conversations. When someone is speaking, there should not be whispering across the table. I often encourage lightening up this explanation to some extent so that you do not appear as a menacing teacher with a ruler in hand. Be firm, but friendly.

As in nearly all social gatherings, there is usually one person (or more) who is much more vocal than the others in the group. And when this person has some wonderful input that appears to be providing reams of quotations for your evaluation, it can be tempting to let the person keep going, even at the cost of other participants' input. Be careful to avoid this. Cut off the "rambler" at a logical break in his or her comments and apologize for doing so. Explain that although the input is proving useful, you need to move on to others in the group and see what they think as well.

At the opposite end of the participant spectrum is the silent person who might nod occasionally or, if feeling a bit more brave, might opt to say, "I agree with what Joe just said" and try to pass that off as his or her entire opinion on the subject. Try not to embarrass these shy participants. Rather, remember to directly ask their opinions on each topic and occasionally ask them *first* so they cannot hide behind other participants' responses. Let them know by your manner and body language that you think what they have to offer is very important to the overall outcome of your study. Lean slightly toward the person who is speaking and look the person in the eye while speaking or when listening to his or her responses.

 Make every participant feel important.

It is not uncommon, given a friendly, lively group of people, to have the conversation get out of hand—either moving off the subject or simply where everyone is talking at once. It is your job as the moderator to restore order to the group without losing the participants' interest. Again, a light touch is usually preferable. You could teasingly restore order by saying something along the line of, "Now class . . ." or remind them that moderating is the closest a market researcher can come to a dictatorship, so you enjoy ordering them to quiet down! Using a humorous tone keeps the group in the mood for continuation of the discussion, while reminding them that they are there for a purpose and on limited time at that.

Another important point for the moderator to remember is that the discussion guide is precisely that, a guide. As one item on your discussion guide is being covered in the conversation, another issue might be mentioned in passing that is not listed on your outline until the middle of the next page. If the comment warrants it and it fits in well, that topic should be covered when it comes up. The idea is to keep the discussion flowing normally rather than in a stilted formal format. Just remember to skip over that item on your discussion guide later if you covered it adequately earlier in the group.

Moderators use different techniques to gather information in focus groups. In addition to straight discussions of topics, participants can be asked to taste-test a new product, play a new computer game, or draw a picture to show how they feel about a topic. Be sure that your methods serve a purpose. What information will you gain from participants' reactions to these types of activities? You have time limitations in a focus group, so you need to use that time wisely.

Consider, for example, a focus group being conducted for a bank. You are a participant and you have just been asked to describe your own bank *as a person*. If your bank were a person, what would he or she look like, how old would he or she be, what hobbies would he or she have, etc. Your responses to this exercise, when viewed in conjunction with those of other respondents, could provide the moderator with valuable image information regarding various financial institutions. Such information can be used in developing advertising, training programs, and so forth. Try responding to this exercise in Worksheet 7–2 to explore whether a similar activity would reveal useful insights for your own focus group topic.

Worksheet 7–2

Instructions: List at least five adjectives to describe your business as a person.

1. _____

2. _____

3. _____

4. _____

5. _____

Finally, and perhaps most important, *do not bias your participants*. Never offer your own opinions on a subject or agree or disagree with any of the comments made by participants during the focus group. The moderator is considered a disinterested bystander. This is the main reason why it is advisable to have someone who does not have an interest in the outcome of the study moderate the related focus groups whenever feasible. It is difficult to moderate a group about, for example, an advertising concept if you yourself developed the concept. There is understandably a temptation to "sell" participants on your opinions. This should be avoided at all costs, or the results of the study will not be reliable. If you are not sure that you can present a nonbiased attitude to the groups, it is highly recommended that you select someone else to moderate your groups.

Paying Participants Co-op Fees

During the recruiting phase of the project you made a decision concerning how to compensate your focus group participants. This compensation, whether it is cash, a gift certificate, or another form of payment, is provided upon completion of each group. It is a common procedure to have participants sign a sheet confirming receipt of their co-op payment. This serves both to alleviate possible complaints of nonpayment as well as to provide you with a record of payments for tax purposes.

It is a normal procedure to recruit extra participants to allow for "no-shows." If more participants show up than are expected, you have two options. Either conduct the groups with all persons who show up or, if you cannot adequately accommodate everyone, select one or two to cancel from the group. You are, in either case, obligated to pay all of the recruits who arrive for your group(s). Those who are asked *not* to participate should be given their co-op payment before they leave and thanked for making the effort to attend.

Analyzing the Results of Focus Group(s)

Analyzing focus group results is different from analyzing survey results. With surveys, your results are quantitative; you have numbers to work with. Focus groups, as explained earlier, provide qualitative results. Your analysis begins by reviewing the tape(s) of your group(s). Note areas where participants strongly agreed or disagreed about an issue. Write down quotations that seem particularly relevant to your study's objectives. Group similar comments to identify participants' preferences. Do not identify any respondent by name in your analysis—respect respondents' confidentiality.

Avoid identifying responses by the number or percentage of respondents making similar statements. Compare differences, for example, between two or more groups, such as customers versus noncustomers. Answers obtained through focus groups are less clear-cut than those from surveys, so concentrate on identifying trends in the responses.

Terms to Remember

Co-op fees Payments made to focus group participants, usually in the form of cash

Confirmation letter Letter sent to person recruited for a focus group to provide directions to the group and serve as a reminder of the time and date of the group

Focus group room Typically a large conference room with a one-way mirror to allow for videotaping and client viewing of the group(s)

Moderator's discussion guide An outline used by a focus group moderator to assist in conducting the discussion in an orderly manner and to ensure that all necessary topics are covered during the group

Qualify To determine through screening questions whether a respondent is the correct person to participate in a study (e.g., the head of the household, 18 years of age or older, etc.)

Recruiting   The process of qualifying and inviting contacts to participate in a focus group

Screener questionnaire   Brief questionnaire used to recruit participants for focus groups or one-on-one interviews

Chapter Eight

Mystery Shopping Programs

Mystery shopping is one of the few market research methodologies that actually sound exciting. As discussed in Chapter 2, mystery shops generally consist of a trained research assistant going into an establishment under the guise of a customer or potential customer to test that company's customer service and sales efforts. Such "shops" are a popular information source for a variety of industries: banks, retail stores, and other service-based companies in particular.

"Shoppers" are trained before conducting the project in order to ensure that they are familiar with situations they might encounter as well as how a company expects their employees to react to various given **scenarios.** Once trained, shoppers conduct their shops by telephone or by in-person visits, depending on the project's specifications. Throughout their shop experience, shoppers are expected to remain alert for all employee reactions during the shop. Items that are monitored frequently include professionalism, courtesy, closing of sales, interest in helping the customer, product knowledge, etc.

Once the shop is completed, the shopper immediately completes a detailed evaluation form while the experience is still fresh in his or her mind. A series of such evaluations are compiled and viewed on an overall basis. This provides an overall service quality picture and can help determine where opportunities exist and where there is room for improvement. Typically, such a project is extended into several waves of shops to allow for comparisons of service over time. In addition, some firms choose to "shop" their competitors to identify where they are exceeding or falling behind their own locations in terms of the issues rated by the shoppers.

A mystery shop program would be appropriate for the owner of a retail shop or several shops who wants to test how well employees are doing on any or all of the following:

- Adhering to return policies
- Approaching customers with a prerequisite greeting
- Selling specific products to meet sales goals
- Closing sales
- Encouraging sales of complementary items (e.g., a scarf to match a dress selection)
- Acting professionally on the sales floor
- Providing accurate information about products

These are just a few examples. A similar situation could arise for a restaurant owner. What types of issues could a mystery shopper evaluate through an in-person visit at a (non–fast food) restaurant? Try to list at least five issues for evaluation in Worksheet 8–1.

Worksheet 8–1

Instructions: List at least five issues that a mystery shopper would evaluate at a (non–fast food) restaurant:

1. _____

2. _____

3. _____

4. _____

5. _____

Some relevant issues for a restaurant mystery shop would include the following:

- Time taken to greet/seat customer
- Recommendations given prior to order being taken
- Additional items suggested (e.g., salad, appetizer) during order-taking process
- Number of times server checked back with customer prior to food being served
- Accuracy of check
- Overall courtesy of server
- Cleanliness/neatness of server (uniform, nails, hair, makeup, etc.)

Quite often other issues are included in mystery shop programs as well. For instance, how easily is your sign viewed from the street? Is your parking easily accessible? How attractive/clean is the outside of your building? What about the inside—is it clean and organized, or is the carpet worn and stained? Basically, this type of program is used to rate a customer's overall experience with your organization. Given all aspects of a visit to your business, how likely would a customer be to come back again?

Steps in Starting Your Own Mystery Shop Program

If your company is service-related, with front-line employees who have regular, ongoing contact with your customers, you might want to consider starting a mystery shop program. Following are the steps necessary to conduct an effective mystery shop:

1. Determine how you will use the results.
2. Design a shop evaluation form.
3. Select the right shoppers.
4. Train your shoppers.
5. Analyze the results.

Determining What You Will Do with the Results

Companies use mystery shop results in a variety of ways, the most common being to develop or enhance employee training. By determining where employees' strengths and weaknesses are, it is easier to determine where training efforts need to be concentrated. Shops can also provide an outsider's view of your shop layout, selection, etc. Comparisons can be made by shopping at your competitors' establishments as well. Some managers use shops as part of their staff incentive programs, with high shop scores resulting in X number of points toward bonuses or prizes. Be careful, however, to keep the focus of the shop program positive.

 Think of mystery shops as a tool, rather than a weapon.

Do not use this program to target negative actions. Rather, use it to reinforce positive ones and to encourage more of the same.

Designing a Shop Evaluation Form

Knowing how you will use the results will help you to identify those areas that you want to be covered in the shop evaluation form. A sample evaluation form for a restaurant is shown in Exhibit 8–1.

Evaluations typically consist of rating items on a specified **scale** to allow for quick, easy-to-relate-to evaluations of shoppers' experiences. An odd-numbered scale (1 to 5 or 1 to 7) is recommended, because it gives a definite midpoint around which to base the ratings of one's shop experience. In addition, as shown in the preceding example, several open-ended questions are generally also asked to allow for explanations of particularly poor or exceptional ratings. Given your own business, assuming that this methodology would be applicable to you, what items would you include in your evaluation form?

Exhibit 8–1

Tony's Restaurant Mystery Shop Program Evaluation Form

Shopper: _____ **Date of visit:** ___ /___ /___

Arrival time: __:__ A.M./P.M. **Departure time:** __:__ A.M./P.M.

Scenario number: _____

****

FACILITY EVALUATION

Q1 How easy was the restaurant to see from the road?

[IF 1 OR 2, EXPLAIN IN SPACE PROVIDED. NOTE THAT "EASY TO SEE" REFERS TO ANY IDENTIFYING FACTORS: THE SIGN, BUILDING ITSELF, ETC.]

	Very Difficult			Very Easy
CIRCLE ONE ONLY:	1	2	3	4	5

[IF 1 OR 2, EXPLAIN:] _____

Q2 How easy was it to enter the parking lot?

	Very Difficult			Very Easy
CIRCLE ONE ONLY:	1	2	3	4	5

[IF 1 OR 2, EXPLAIN:] _____

Q3 Was parking available?

( ) Yes

( ) No

(Continued)

Exhibit 8–1 (Continued)

HOST/HOSTESS EVALUATION

Q4 How long did you wait before you were approached by the host/hostess?

( ) No wait at all/approached immediately

( ) Less than 1 minute

( ) 1–2 minutes

( ) 3–5 minutes

( ) 6–10 minutes

( ) Over 10 minutes

Q5 How many people were waiting in front of you when you arrived?

Number waiting: _____

Q6 Did the host/hostess smile when greeting you?

( ) Yes

( ) No

Q7 Did he or she do any of the following? [CHECK ALL THAT APPLY]

( ) Indicate how long you would have to wait to be seated

( ) Ask how many in your party

( ) Ask if you wanted the nonsmoking section

Q8 Rate the host/hostess on the following aspects:

	Poor				Excellent
a. Professional appearance	1	2	3	4	5
b. Greeting	1	2	3	4	5
c. Courtesy	1	2	3	4	5
d. Efficiency	1	2	3	4	5
e. Interest in helping you	1	2	3	4	5

(Continued)

Exhibit 8–1 (Continued)

WAITSTAFF EVALUATION

Q9 How long did you wait after being seated until the waiter/waitress approached your table?

( ) No wait at all/approached immediately

( ) Less than 1 minute

( ) 1–2 minutes

( ) 3–5 minutes

( ) 6–10 minutes

( ) Over 10 minutes

Q10 Did the waiter/waitress introduce himself or herself?

( ) Yes

( ) No

Q11 Did he or she smile?

( ) Yes

( ) No

Q12 Did he or she interrupt you?

( ) Yes

( ) No

Q13 Did he or she do any of the following? [CHECK ALL THAT APPLY]

( ) Offer suggestions/favorites for meal

( ) Identify daily specials

( ) Offer crackers, crayons, etc., for children

( ) Ask if you would like to first order a drink or appetizer

( ) Bring dessert tray out prior to bringing bill to table

(Continued)

Exhibit 8–1 (Continued)

Q14 Rate the waiter/waitress on the following aspects:

	Poor				Excellent
a. Professional appearance	1	2	3	4	5
b. Getting order correct	1	2	3	4	5
c. Efficiency	1	2	3	4	5
d. Courtesy	1	2	3	4	5
e. Greeting	1	2	3	4	5
f. Menu knowledge	1	2	3	4	5
g. Sales effort	1	2	3	4	5

FOOD EVALUATION

Q15 Rate the food on the following aspects:

	Poor				Excellent
a. Presentation	1	2	3	4	5
b. Temperature	1	2	3	4	5
c. Taste	1	2	3	4	5
d. Freshness	1	2	3	4	5
e. Value for price	1	2	3	4	5
f. Portion size	1	2	3	4	5

OVERALL EVALUATION

Q16 Based on your experience during this visit, how likely would you be to visit this restaurant again?

	Not Likely				Very Likely
CIRCLE ONE RATING:	1	2	3	4	5

(Continued)

Selecting the Right Shoppers

Once you have determined what you want to evaluate, you need to profile what you consider to be an average customer in your store (or whatever your business is). Shoppers need to be representative of the average person who could come through your front door. If you normally cater to high-income businesspeople, your shoppers should "look the part." Likewise, if you generally deal with the "twentysomething" crowd interested in particular clothing trends, your shoppers should fit this profile. Also remember to recruit enough shoppers so that the same shopper does not go to the same site repeatedly.

When conducting a mystery shop program on your own, it is important to remember that the shoppers should not be people with whom your staff is familiar. For example, employees are likely to treat the manager's spouse with a more deferential attitude than other customers. If he or she were conducting a shop, this might result in higher than normal ratings that would not necessarily be a true representation of your service levels. Likewise, past employees or friends of current employees would not be good choices for shoppers. They are probably somewhat biased toward your company. Also, they might, however inadvertently, suggest that they are conducting a shop, thereby defeating the entire process. You might want to consider hiring college students or retirees to "shop" for you. This would cost less than an outside vendor, but remember the training time involved if you choose to go this route.

Training Your Shoppers

If a vendor is conducting your shops, the project manager or outside field supervisor will typically handle briefing and training the shoppers for you. Assuming still that you are handling the shop program yourself, you will need to set some time aside to discuss the program with your shoppers. If possible, all shoppers should be trained at the same time. Review the shop evaluation form with them question by question. Encourage the shoppers to ask questions or discuss items they are unsure of or possibly uncomfortable with. Emphasize the need for honesty and unbiased evaluations.

It is important to remind shoppers not to take the evaluation forms, shop instructions, or other similar materials into a facility when conducting their shops. Evaluations should be completed immediately following the shops, off the property and out of view of the staff. Shoppers should use their own names, addresses, and phone numbers if a shop scenario is likely to require employees to follow up with them.

It is also important to review each shopper's scenarios. What specifically are they to purchase, ask for, etc.? They should familiarize themselves with these scenarios before conducting their shop(s). Shoppers can have different scenarios, so they should somehow indicate the scenario used at the top of each evaluation form.

Analyzing Mystery Shop Results

When looking at the completed mystery shop evaluation forms, keep in mind that this type of study is more qualitative than quantitative in nature. Shops are "snapshots" of service at the points in time that the shoppers make their visits or calls. They are not necessarily indicative of an overall service, but they can serve as a barometer of how things are going.

If a number of shoppers mention problems with, for example, long waits to be seated at Tony's Restaurant, there are a few ways of looking at this issue. First, check to see if all of the shops occurred at typical rush times such as lunch or dinner. If so, this may simply be a function of people with reservations arriving early or people not making reservations at all. This could be alleviated, for example, by additional host staffing at these times or strong encouragement of reservations for dining at these times. If, however, the shops occurred at a wide variety of times, it might indicate a training issue for hosts or waitstaff in terms of improving time management and efficiency.

Look at the shops on an overall basis. Pay close attention to any comments offered by the shoppers. Avoid singling out employees or individual situations. Instead, look for trends in the shop results. Often mystery shop results are compiled in tables using the coding and tabulation techniques discussed in Chapter 5. This provides an easier way to look at the overall results and spot trends in the shoppers' experiences. Remember when doing this, however, to avoid looking at percentages, because the bases are typically small and the shops are not conducted based on a statistical sampling.

Terms to Remember

Scale A specified range of numbers assigned to qualitative terms to allow numerical assessment of a quality or issue

Scenarios Predetermined situations used by mystery shoppers to evaluate staff reactions

Chapter Nine

Quality Control in Market Research

This book thus far has operated under the credo that "Some research is better than no research." If you are not careful when conducting and analyzing your research, your solutions can simply become new problems. Following are six ways to ensure the quality of your research efforts:

1. Test your questionnaire.
2. Put checks on sample quality.
3. Train your interviewers.
4. Edit and validate questionnaires.
5. Know your vendor's quality procedures.
6. Check your final results.

Testing Your Questionnaire

Proofread your questionnaire carefully. Check wording to be sure it is clear and easy to understand. Follow through each question, testing possible responses to ensure that it flows well and that the right people are being asked the right questions. Ask at least one other person to also review the questionnaire and, if at all possible, pretest your questionnaire with qualified respondents.

In Tony's case, for example, he could test the customer version of his questionnaire with 5–10 customers to see whether they can easily complete it and to determine how much time it takes. A mail survey is hard to test; it is recommended that you ask persons outside of your business to review and respond to the survey to test the flow. With a telephone survey, typically a number of calls (again, 5–10 would suffice) are made to test the flow and respondents' understanding of exactly what you are asking them.

Checking Sample Quality

Again, remember that it is just as important to find the right person to survey as it is to ask the right questions. Even when you are convinced that your sample is up-to-date and accurate, force yourself to be somewhat pessimistic. Allow for discrepancies in the lists and circumvent them by making sure you check all qualifications with screener questions at the beginning of your survey or recruiting effort. Frequently used screeners relate to respondents' ages, where they live, and usage frequency (i.e., how often they come into your establishment or purchase a certain product). These questions will help to guarantee that you survey the correct people—those whose responses will be pertinent to your decision-making process.

Training Interviewers

You need to train thoroughly anyone who will conduct a telephone survey for you. Even professional interviewers receive a briefing on a questionnaire for a new project. Be thorough in your explanation of the survey. At a minimum, be sure to cover the following issues:

- Why you are conducting the survey
- Who they will be interviewing
- How the survey "reads" (Read through the entire questionnaire, covering all skip patterns, when to read or not to read response lists, etc.)

- Basic interview expectations: courtesy, confidentiality, probing and clarifying, and question rotation

Finally, encourage a role-playing exercise, in which interviewers pair off and take turns representing interviewers and respondents. This allows them an opportunity to get comfortable with the survey and the correct way to record responses.

 All interviewers must receive the same training to ensure consistency in how survey questions are asked and answered.

Audiotape your interviewer briefing session. Then, if an interviewer misses the initial training session, he or she will be able to get the same information as those who did attend. Above all, encourage interviewers to ask questions. If the interviewer is unsure about how to *ask* a question, the respondent will certainly be confused about how to *answer* it.

Editing and Validating Questionnaires

If you are conducting a telephone survey, spot-check completed questionnaires to make sure that:

- Respondents understand what is being asked.
- Interviewers complete the questionnaires correctly.

All completed surveys should be edited as a check on skip patterns and indicated instructions for survey completion (e.g., that only one item is checked where one response is requested or that verbatim comments are presented in complete sentences). You might also want to **validate** responses by arranging a second phone call to a few respondents and asking key questions a second time to ascertain that interviewers are recording responses correctly. Although validation is frequently used as a quality check on field personnel at research firms, it might not prove either necessary or cost-effective for your own in-house studies.

Understanding Vendors' Quality Procedures

References from past clients are important when selecting a vendor, but such referrals are not always representative of the quality you can expect. Think about it—would *you* put a poor reference on your resume? If you are contracting with an outside vendor to conduct your research, ask up front what types of quality controls they have established. How will they guarantee the quality of their work?

Ask about their interviewer **monitoring** process. Do supervisors periodically listen to random interviews to ensure that they are going well? Discuss their interviewer and supervisor training procedures. If a vendor indicates that they offer interviewer incentives, ask for details about how their program works. If it is based solely on the number of interviews completed on a shift, think twice. Such programs tend to encourage rushed interviews, sloppy responses, and short verbatim quotations from respondents. Better incentive plans are those that reward interviewers for consistent quality in their work, such as the number of completed surveys that proved error-free in editing.

Also, do not hesitate to request that you join the staff for the interviewer briefing and be allowed to monitor initial interviews yourself. Most research facilities are equipped with monitoring equipment that allows you to listen in on an interview without being heard by either the respondent or the interviewer. All of these aspects will help you to ensure that you have selected the right firm for the job.

Checking Your Final Results

Tabulating surveys manually is a tedious job and as such is prone to human error. Whether you tabulate your surveys or have someone in your business do so for you, before finalizing and analyzing the results, tally all columns at least a second time to ensure that it all adds up. Likewise, double-check the percentage figures. Wrong numbers can provide wrong data, which ultimately leads to wrong decisions.

Even data entry and programming personnel at outside vendors can make mistakes. Carefully proofread your tables even if they are done by a research vendor or data processing firm. Spot-check accuracy by adding up selected columns. Also check questions that are affected by skip patterns in the questionnaire to be sure that the correct respondents answered the correct questions. If you have questions, call your vendor and ask them to explain those areas that concern you.

Terms to Remember

Monitoring Listening to survey interviews to determine if interviewers are conducting the survey correctly and to ascertain that respondents are correctly interpreting the questions asked

Validate Calling back a respondent and repeating key survey questions to ascertain that interviewers are correctly recording responses

Chapter Ten

Selecting and Working with a Research Vendor

Steps in Cost-Effective Vendor Relationships

Research needs can arise suddenly. Small-business owners often have time or staff limitations that prevent them from conducting an entire project in-house. Rather than assuming that conducting research through an outside vendor will be too expensive, consider the following ways to make outside research cost-effective:

1. Identify vendors with reasonable costs.
2. Develop objectives.
3. Prepare a request for proposal.
4. Review proposals and meet with vendors.
5. Communicate effectively with vendors.
6. Avoid overqualifying respondents.

Identifying Vendors with Reasonable Costs

First, identify at least three research firms (or consultants) in your area. Selecting candidates from the local Yellow Pages is one option, but it is preferable to ask your business associates to recommend firms or call your Chamber of Commerce and ask for member firms.

Developing Objectives

Before contacting the vendors, write down what you consider to be the objectives of the proposed research—what you want to find out (see Chapter 1). Also identify what resources are available in-house. Even if you do not have time to conduct the study, take the time to pull all available information together. Do you have customer lists with names, telephone numbers, and addresses? Do you have copies of previous studies or additional information on your company that you can provide to the vendors so they can better understand your current status?

You should develop a list of potential questions for the study (see Chapter 4). Based on the objectives you have identified, what would you like to ask customers, noncustomers, etc.? This list need not be in any assemblance of order, nor do you have to word the questions exactly as they would appear on a questionnaire or in a focus group discussion guide. What this list does accomplish is to reduce the amount of time required by a research vendor for the development of your questionnaire. The actual research tool will add or delete questions from your original list, but such a list provides a good starting point.

Preparing the Request for Proposal

When you have compiled a summary of internal information sources, objectives, and questions, put this information into a letter format. Send identical letters to each of the vendors you have selected. Identify who you are, in general what your objectives are, and what sample lists, company information, etc., you would be able to provide them with. Also indicate when the results of the proposed study are expected to be needed.

This letter is referred to as an **RFP** or **request for proposal.** In it you should also request background information (qualifications) for personnel who would work on your project as well as several references, particularly for work done for firms of your size or in your industry. Once the vendors have received your letter, they should respond in writing by recommending a methodology and providing an estimated cost for your proposed project.

A poor response to your RFP (spelling errors, poor addition of cost figures, slow response time, etc.) should be a warning flag to consider a different vendor.

Reviewing Proposals and Meeting with Vendors

When reviewing proposals, bear in mind that there could be more than one method that would provide you with the information you require. Be willing to consider various methodologies. Also, take the time to call references and ask how well these vendors met other clients' needs. Did they meet deadlines? Did they stay within set budget guidelines? Were they responsive to the clients' needs?

If time allows, meet with the vendor(s) who appear to be offering you the best option(s). Note that this meeting should be considered a sales effort on the vendor's part, so you should not be charged for it. During your meeting with the sales representative, project manager, and/or consultant, consider the following checklist:

- Has the vendor ever worked with firms in your industry before? If so, what types of studies have they conducted?

- What is the project manager's background, and what types of clients does he or she typically serve (size, industry, methodologies, etc.)?

- Who would be your primary contact? Is there a good rapport with this person in the initial meeting?

- Why did the vendor specifically recommend a certain methodology? Are there other options?

- Does the vendor representative ask you specific questions and appear interested in working on the project?

- What are their hourly rates for different aspects of the work (design, interviewing, coding, data processing, reporting, word processing, focus group moderation, etc.)? How does their original estimate break down?

- Are they willing to work within budget guidelines (e.g., cut design costs if you give them your lists of questions or use an in-house conference room for a focus group)? (This should be the very *last* item discussed.)

It is crucial to find a vendor who will work with you to meet your needs. Be open, however, to the consultant's possible recommendations against certain requests. You still want to ensure the integrity of your final research results. Ask the vendor to explain why something will or will not work.

Communicating with Vendors

When the project is in its development stages, keep the lines of communication open with the vendor. Answer his or her questions and provide information promised in a timely manner. At your planning session, it is advisable to develop a final project schedule as well as a task distribution list that clearly identifies the vendor's responsibilities and your own. An example of such a list for a telephone survey of customers is shown in Exhibit 10–1.

When reporting is completed, your vendor should also be able to provide you with recommendations based on the findings of the survey. Do not hesitate to insist on this; this expertise is one of the main reasons you would want to use an outside vendor. Reporting

---

Exhibit 10–1

Division of Responsibility between Clients and Vendors

Client	Vendor
• Provide survey objectives	• Develop survey questionnaire
• Provide input into questionnaire development	• Conduct interviewer briefing
• Provide telephone list of customers	• Conduct survey interviews
• Attend survey briefing/monitor initial interviews	• Provide coding, data tabulation, and survey analysis/report

---

should not simply reiterate the percentage of responses to questions 1 through 20; rather, it should tell you how to use this information to meet your initially stated objectives.

If the project runs over the course of several months, ask for periodic updates to ensure that the schedule is meeting your expectations and needs. Updates could be conducted briefly by telephone or simply consist of a faxed summary updating completed interviews, reporting status, etc.

Avoiding Overqualification

Finally, be aware that cost overruns can occur when conducting research studies. If you revise your questionnaire, particularly by adding questions, you change the length of interviewing time involved and therefore increase the costs involved. The more detailed your requirements for qualifying respondents or focus group participants, the higher the costs will be. For example, it could be relatively inexpensive to survey women between the ages of 25 and 45. The incidence of these respondents will be fairly high. It becomes more difficult, however, to identify and survey women in that same age group who are divorced, have MBA degrees, and eat out three times a week—the incidence of your potential respondents has decreased dramatically. If you overqualify respondents, your costs increase substantially, as does the time involved in conducting the study.

Ethical Considerations in Vendor Relationships

Ethics are important when dealing with an outside vendor. Just as you expect your vendors to be straightforward with you, they also expect certain behavior. Do not ask vendors to provide prices simply because a manager would like an extra bid in the file if the contract is about to be awarded to another vendor. Unless you sincerely will consider the **bids** you request, it is unfair to expect a vendor to put the necessary hours into preparing a proposal without hope of winning the contract. Likewise, do not offer to give a vendor "all of your research" in exchange for a "deal" on your current study. It is not a given that the work will be there "next time," and it is unfair to take advantage of the vendor. (This does not, however, preclude you from asking for an itemization of the vendor's prices and discussing how they are arrived at—both sides need to deal fairly with each other.) The key to research ethics, as with any business relationship, is to treat research vendors with the same courtesy, honesty, and professionalism that you would expect in return from them.

Terms to Remember

Bid A written proposal from a research vendor, including costs, submitted in response to an RFP

Request for Proposal (RFP) A formal letter to research vendors identifying research needs and asking them to respond with recommended methodologies and estimated pricing

RFP See **Request for Proposal**

Chapter **Eleven**

"Making or Breaking" Your Research Budget

When developing a research project, it is important to be aware of the various factors that can affect your cost levels, either negatively or positively. In a telephone survey, for example, anything that increases the amount of time devoted to the project is going to increase the project costs accordingly.

Telephone Surveys

Following are factors involved in determining the costs for a telephone survey as well as suggestions for reducing your costs.

Questionnaire Length

The more time your interviewers spend with respondents on the phone, the more costly your survey will be: not only because of the expense represented by the interviewers, but also because of increases in long-distance costs and the data processing that will need to be done once the survey is completed. Keep your questionnaire concise. Do not attempt to cover unrelated topics in the survey and ask only for information that you have a use for; "nice to know" items, generally speaking, are a waste of time and money.

Incidence of Qualified Respondents

The cost of your survey will be determined, in part, by the incidence, or rate of occurrence in the population, of potential respondents. If you are interviewing any consumer in the state over the age of 18, it will be relatively simple to find potential respondents. If, however, you need to talk to single mothers over the age of 30 who make over $50,000 per year, you will have a more difficult time locating respondents. In other words, the more difficult your criteria make it to qualify a respondent, the higher your survey costs will be.

Number of Interviews

Your costs will increase with the number of interviews you conduct. Each interview requires interviewing time, editing, coding, data processing, and, depending on the scope of the study, long-distance costs. Therefore, with each interview, costs can be expected to rise at least slightly. Determine what sample size provides you with the appropriate statistical reliability. Unless you are doing extensive cross-tabulations of the data or need to look in detail at specific quota groups within the overall respondent base, doing more interviews than statistically necessary is "overkill" and can cost you unnecessary dollars.

Timing

The timing of a survey can also affect your project costs. If you conduct a telephone survey during December you risk losing potential respondents due to the holiday season. When people are out shopping, going to parties and visiting families, it is difficult to catch them by phone and even more difficult to persuade them to respond to a survey! Sunday is typically a bad day for interviewing as are three-day weekends. And, by all means, avoid calling respondents after 8:30 in the evening.

Executive Interviews

It is important to recognize that businesspersons are far more difficult to reach and interview than other respondents. A more detailed series of screeners is required to reach a businessperson, and, frequently, the respondent does not have time to answer all your questions—a fact that often necessitates call backs (and additional expense).

Pretesting the Questionnaire

While a pretest of the questionnaire can raise your project's costs slightly, in the long run it can save money: first, by ensuring that all your questionnaire is easily understood by the respondents; and, second, by giving you "advance warning" about any problems relating to the length of the questionnaire. After pretesting, you will be able to clarify any questions that have proven to be too vague and/or reduce the number of questions to maintain a workable interview length.

Open-Ended Questions

Open-ended questions can increase costs by requiring interviewers to type (or frequently write out by hand) verbatim responses to questions. Additionally, in those instances where the open-ended responses will be coded to provide a database table, the cost of the coding becomes a factor. The more open-ended questions in the survey, the greater the costs associated with coding will be.

Mail Surveys

As with telephone surveys, certain aspects need to be given careful consideration when developing a mail survey.

Questionnaire Length

The longer the survey, the more data entry and data processing time will be involved. Also, if a survey is too lengthy, it can have a negative effect on your response rate by "scaring off" potential respondents. If your response rate is too low, a second mailing may be required, thereby further raising the cost of the survey (additional printing and postage).

First-Class Postage

If survey results are urgently required, it may be necessary to mail your surveys out by first-class mail. If, however, your survey is simply an annual customer satisfaction study, third-class or bulk-rate postage might suffice.

Printing

The format the survey takes also affects costs. If you can reduce the number of pages on a mail survey, you may encourage a higher response rate. In addition, the more detailed and lengthy the questionnaire, the higher the actual printing costs. As with the telephone survey, be sure that you are asking only those questions you really need the answers to.

Return Postage

When conducting a mail survey, always provide return postage for survey respondents. While this item might seem like a logical cost-cutter, failure to provide it can negatively affect your survey response rate by discouraging potential respondents.

Focus Groups

Focus groups also have factors which should be considered in a research project budget.

Number of Groups

The number of groups that you conduct will affect your costs. The more groups conducted, the higher the costs of recruiting. In addition, increased groups call for increased refreshment costs and co-op fees. Remember, however, vendors and hotels often charge by the night for a conference room rental, making two groups more cost-effective. Typically, at least two focus groups are recommended for a study.

Location of Groups

While a formal group facility is always preferable, it may often be more than you have budgeted if you are handling the study yourself. Consider other options such as a hotel meeting room, a conference room in your office building, a local restaurant banquet room, etc., in order to find a more cost-effective location to meet your needs. Provided that you can tape the groups and that there will not be loud distractions (such as a band at a restaurant) such options can work well for focus groups.

Co-op Fees

Participants should always receive something for their time, and cash is generally the best motivator. The "going" rates are $35 to $40 for consumers and $75 or more for executives and professionals (these standard amounts may vary by region, so check with a local vendor for local rates). If such fees are not in your range, consider gift certificates, free services, etc., to provide motivation for recruits to attend. Be sure to tell them what you will be giving them to instill a reason for attending. Remember that anyone who shows up on time for the groups must receive compensation. If more people show than you have room for, you should compensate anyone who arrived and was turned away. Always remember to figure in the "co-op" for participants when developing a focus group study budget.

Case One

Nonprofit Organization

Identifying Research Needs

City Lights, a local nonprofit organization, coordinates a crisis center, homeless shelter, and childcare center. With ever-increasing costs, its Board of Directors wanted to determine how the organization could increase donations and, perhaps even more importantly, how it could increase *repeat* donations from past donors. Board members agreed that market research on this subject was needed to get reliable information. To decrease the potentially negative impact on City Lights' already tight budget, the members agreed to develop and conduct the research study (or studies) themselves.

Determining Objectives

At an initial "brainstorming" session, the Board members reviewed what they believed to be important information. They wanted to learn, of course, what factors prompt people to donate. All of the Board members *believed* they had an idea of how people make their charitable donation decisions, but, given their own obvious biases on this topic, they realized that they needed to evaluate this issue with greater certainty. The kinds of issues that needed clarification included:

- Do people offer donations out of a sense of duty?
- Is donating connected to an emotional bond to the organization?
- What about peer pressure? Does that play a role?
- Do people typically donate because they are contacted during specific fund-raising events?

The Board also wanted to find out how donors/potential donors have heard about City Lights. What effect does word-of-mouth have on the community's awareness of the organization? How successful have their public relations efforts been? How effective are direct mail campaigns for nonprofit organizations? Likewise, it was very important for the Board to learn *how* people donate to non-profits: timing, selected donation amounts, and the form(s) their donations actually take (i.e., cash, credit cards, checks, donated equipment or supplies, volunteered time, etc.).

By the conclusion of their meeting, the Board of Directors had compiled a list of objectives for their research. Following are the objectives that they planned to work on:

1. Identify frequency and timing of charitable contributions, both to City Lights, as well as to others.
2. Measure annual donation amounts (average donations to various nonprofit organizations).
3. Determine donors' preferred uses for their donated funds. Do they designate specific uses within an organization for their donations?
4. Evaluate *how* donors prefer to make their donations (i.e., cash, credits, specifically donated items such as equipment or supplies, volunteered time, etc.)
5. Measure awareness of the organization within its market/ service area.
6. Evaluate the effectiveness of the organization's communication efforts (both "internally" with regular donors and "externally" with prospective donors).
7. Develop a donor profile in terms of demographics (income, education level, age, occupation, etc.) as well as in terms of their media viewing/listening/reading habits.

One Board member suggested that they should also consider including corporate donors within the scope of the proposed research. While all agreed that this is an important concern, most felt that City Lights' current corporate outreach program was doing a thorough and effective job of reaching area businesses and encouraging donations. Thus, they chose to concentrate their research efforts solely on the public sector.

Selecting a Methodology

At their next planning session, the Board members discussed the possible means of gathering the information they required. It was suggested that they should initially consult with their contacts at other similar nonprofit organizations to seek input for their research development process. If similar research had been done through one or more of those organizations, then they might be able to gain insights to be used in developing their own study. Two Board members were assigned to this fact-finding effort. Once that aspect was completed, they expected that they would then be able to determine the most appropriate methodology for their own study.

One week later, the designated Board members reported back with suggestions from several other nonprofit organizations. Each organization had tried, with varying degrees of success, to research its markets in terms of donors. As might be expected, limited budgets had dictated what could be accomplished. One group had conducted focus groups, but had experienced a great deal of difficulty in recruiting participants because they expected to be given a "pitch" for donations and were leery of the sponsor's motives.

Another organization had attempted to conduct a telephone survey, but had tied it into their telephone pledge drive. They reported a dismally low response rate. If people were donating, they wanted to donate and get off the phone. If they were contacted and chose *not* to donate, then the survey almost seemed accusatory in tone: "Why do you choose not to donate to nonprofit organizations?"

A representative from an area food bank suggested the importance of avoiding any type of primary research close to major holiday times, particularly Thanksgiving or Christmas. Potential respondents are typically flooded with mail and "pleas" for charitable donations. As a result, response rates are lower than they might be at other times of the year.

Nevertheless, some of the results that these organizations had obtained from their research would be helpful to the Board when designing its own questionnaire. After reviewing the input from their colleagues, the Board of Directors selected a mail survey as their research methodology. With this method, they could copy questionnaires in-house and mail them out at a minimal cost with their postal permit. Two questions needed resolution:

1. Whether or not postage-paid return envelopes should be included with the questionnaires.
2. Whether or not City Lights should be identified as the sponsor of the survey.

Members decided to include postage-paid envelopes for the respondents' convenience to encourage a higher rate of responses to the survey. They also decided to *not* specifically identify City Lights as the sponsor of the survey but would, in selected questions, include the organization among the pre-coded responses. It was felt that this "blind" survey would serve a dual purpose:

1. It should encourage more honest comments and input from the respondents.
2. It would avoid alienating regular donors who might become annoyed by the use of the organization's funds, no matter how small, for such a study.

Identifying Respondents

The next step was to clearly identify who the organization would survey. Given the research objectives, it was apparent that they required input from both those people who *had* donated to City Lights and those who had *not*. Lists of all donors for the past five years were readily available on the in-house database. The director of the study drew samples from two specific groups of donors: those who had donated during the past 12 months and those who were identified as donors within the past five years, but not during the past 12 months. This would allow the organization to determine both why people decide to donate *and* why they may stop donating to nonprofit organizations. Because the Board viewed donations as a very personal decision, they decided that they would survey on a per capita basis rather than mailing questionnaires to *households*. The reasoning for this decision was based on the knowledge that many of their donations have come from within a single household. For instance, a father, son, and daughter, each residing at the same household, might each make their *own* individual donations to a given organization. Past experience had shown this to be a frequent occurrence.

Although the organization's current donor base was understandably smaller than the five-year donor base, they managed to compile a list of 1,500. A randomized list of 1,500 past donors was also compiled from all persons who had donated within the previous five years. To reach *nondonors*, the Board arranged to purchase a random listing of 2,000 area residents (all within a specified grouping of local Zip codes). As the same questionnaire was expected to be used for each of the three populations being surveyed, the Board was not particularly concerned with any possible overlap of names on any of the sample lists. It would be unlikely that anyone would mistakenly complete the same questionnaire more than one time.

Questionnaire Development

With the objectives determined, the methodology selected and sample available, the Board next set to work developing their questionnaire. Using their objectives as guidelines, they developed an outline from which they would be able to design the actual questionnaire (Exhibit C–1).

Once the basic outline for the questionnaire was established, the actual writing of the questionnaire was now simplified. The survey instrument is shown in Exhibit C–2.

Exhibit C-1

Donor Survey Outline

I. Survey Introduction

II. Awareness of Nonprofit Organizations

    A. Local Organizations?

        1. Which ones?

        2. How heard of?

    B. Other Organizations (National, International, etc.)

        1. Which ones?

        2. How heard of?

III. Monetary Charitable Donations

    A. Ever made monetary donations?

        1. Yes

            a. To what organization(s)?

            b. Why chose organization(s)?

            c. How often?

            d. Average amount?

            e. Preferred donation method?

            f. Anything that would encourage more frequent or larger donations?

                1. Yes - what?

                2. No - why not?

        2. No

            a. Why not?

            b. What would encourage donations?

            c. If were to donate, to what organization(s) most likely?

                1. Why?

            d. Preferred donation method?

(Continued)

Exhibit C-1 (Continued)

B. Ever done volunteer work?

  1. Yes

    a. Type of volunteer work?

    b. For what organization(s)?

    c. Why chose organization(s)?

    d. How often?

    e. Anything that would encourage additional volunteer work?

      1. Yes - what?

      2. No - why not?

  2. No

    a. Why not?

    b. What would encourage volunteerism?

    c. If did volunteer, most likely with which organization(s)?

      1. Why?

  3. Ever participate in fund-raising activities?

    a. Yes

      1. Specific event(s)?

      2. When?

      3. What prompted?

      4. What was your role?

      5. Anything that would encourage additional participation?

        a. Yes - what?

        b. No - why not?

IV. Donor Profit

  A. Media

    1. Television Habits

      a. Channels viewed?

      b. Show types viewed?

      c. Usual viewing times?

(Continued)

Exhibit C–1 (Continued)

2. Radio Habits

    a. Stations listened to?

    b. Programming types listened to?

    c. Usual listening times?

3. Newspaper Readership

    a. Newspapers read?

    b. Frequency?

    c. Specific sections, all or skim?

4. Transit/Outdoor

    a. Regular commute habits?

        1. Auto

        2. Transit - bus/subway

        3. Bike

        4. Car/vanpool

    b. Time spent in commute?

    c. Notice billboards/transit ads?

B. Advertising Effects

1. Read direct mail?

    a. Why?

    b. Why not?

2. Watch TV ads?

    a. Why?

    b. Why not?

3. Listen to radio ads?

    a. Why?

    b. Why not?

4. Notice outdoor ads?

    a. Why?

    b. Why not?

(Continued)

Exhibit C-1

   C.   Demographics
1. Age?
2. Education Level?
3. Income Range?
4. Number of Children under 18?
5. Home Ownership?
6. Occupation?
7. Number of Years Living in Area?
8. Home ZIP Code?
9. Gender

Exhibit C-2

Nonprofit Awareness Survey

Dear Neighbor:

In an effort to evaluate charitable giving efforts in our community, this survey is being conducted. You are one of many people in the area who are being contacted to give input on the current state of nonprofit organizations and public awareness of them. Please take a few minutes to give your input and comments. Your responses will be kept confidential and you will not be contacted for donations from any nonprofit organizations due to your participation in this survey. Thank you!

****

Q1 Are you personally aware of any nonprofit organizations in your community or in the immediately surrounding area?

    1 - ( ) Yes ——> [CONTINUE TO Q2]

    2 - ( ) No ——> [SKIP TO Q3a]

Q2 Which organizations have you heard of? [RECORD ALL ORGANIZATIONS BELOW]

_____

_____

_____

_____

Q3 How did you learn about the organization(s) you listed above? [CHECK ALL THAT APPLY]

    1 - ( ) Through a friend/family member

    2 - ( ) Once utilized their services

    3 - ( ) Received direct mail from them

    4 - ( ) Attended/heard of a fund-raiser

    5 - ( ) Saw television ad

    6 - ( ) Saw item about them on the news

(Continued)

Exhibit C–2 (Continued)

7 - ( ) Read article about them in newspaper

8 - ( ) Saw newspaper advertisement

9 - ( ) Did volunteer work there

10 - ( ) Heard news about them on radio

11 - ( ) Heard radio advertisement

12 - ( ) My employer donates to them

13 - ( ) Other [SPECIFY: _____]

14 - ( ) Don't know/don't recall

Q3a What other nonprofit organizations, if any, have you heard of? [THESE CAN BE AT A STATE, NATIONAL OR INTERNATIONAL LEVEL. PLEASE LIST ALL WHICH YOU ARE AWARE OF.]

_____

_____

_____

Q4 And how did you hear of the organization(s) you listed above [FROM Q3a]? [CHECK ALL THAT APPLY BELOW.]

1 - ( ) Through a friend/family member

2 - ( ) Once utilized their services

3 - ( ) Received direct mail through them

4 - ( ) Attended/heard of a fund-raiser

5 - ( ) Saw television ad

6 - ( ) Saw item about them on the news

7 - ( ) Read article about them in newspaper

8 - ( ) Saw newspaper advertisement

9 - ( ) Did volunteer work there

10 - ( ) Heard about them on radio

11 - ( ) Heard radio advertisement

12 - ( ) My employer donates to them

13 - ( ) Other [SPECIFY: _____]

14 - ( ) Don't know/don't recall

(Continued)

Exhibit C–2 (Continued)

Q5 Have you ever made monetary donations to a non-charitable organization?

    1 - ( ) Yes ——> [CONTINUE TO Q6]

    2 - ( ) No ——> [SKIP TO Q13]

Q6 To which organizations have you donated? [LIST BELOW.]

_____

_____

_____

Q7 Why did you choose this/these organization(s) to donate to? [CHECK ALL THAT APPLY BELOW]

    1 - ( ) I/a friend/a family member had utilized/are using services

    2 - ( ) Recommended by my church/synagogue

    3 - ( ) They have a good reputation/are well-known

    4 - ( ) They were conducting a fund-raiser/pledge drive

    5 - ( ) It is a cause in which I believe/am interested

    6 - ( ) I always donate to them

    7 - ( ) They are important to my community/perform needed service

    8 - ( ) Other [SPECIFY: _____

        _____

        _____

    9 - ( ) Don't recall why originally decided to donate

Q8 How often would you say you usually make monetary donations to any of the nonprofit organizations that you have mentioned? [CHECK ONE ONLY BELOW. NOTE THAT MONETARY REFERS TO CASH, CHECK, PLEDGED DOLLARS OR CREDIT CARDS]

    1 - ( ) Weekly

    2 - ( ) Monthly

    3 - ( ) Quarterly (every 3 months)

(Continued)

Exhibit C–2 (Continued)

4 - ( ) Annually

5 - ( ) Varies by non-profit [PLEASE GIVE ANSWER BASED ON OVERALL DONATIONS TO ALL CHARITIES]

6 - ( ) Don't know/unsure

Q9 When did you make your most recent monetary donation? [CHECK ONE ONLY BELOW]

1 - ( ) Within the past week

2 - ( ) Within the past month

3 - ( ) Within the past three months

4 - ( ) Within the past six months

5 - ( ) Within the past year

6 - ( ) Within the past two years

7 - ( ) Between two and five years ago

8 - ( ) Don't recall/unsure

9 - ( ) Other [SPECIFY: _____]

Q10 And what would you estimate is your *average* donation each time you donate to a nonprofit organization? [ESTIMATE DOLLAR AMOUNT BASED ON AVERAGE ONE-TIME DONATION]

1 - ( ) EST. AVG. DONATION: $ __ __ __ , __ __ __ . __ __

2 - ( ) Don't know

Q11 When making monetary donations to nonprofit organizations, what is your preferred method of payment? [CHECK ONE BELOW - *MOST* PREFERRED]

1 - ( ) Cash

2 - ( ) Personal check

3 - ( ) Cashier's check or money order

4 - ( ) Credit card

5 - ( ) Pledge and make payment on billing schedule

(Continued)

Exhibit C–2 (Continued)

6 - ( ) Automatic deduction from paycheck

7 - ( ) Other [SPECIFY: _____]

8 - ( ) No preference

9 - ( ) Don't know/unsure

Q12 Is there anything that the nonprofit(s) you donate to could do to encourage you to donate more or more frequently?

    1 - ( ) Yes ——> [SPECIFY: _____

            _____

            _____

            _____]

    2 - ( ) No [SPECIFY WHY NOT: _____

            _____

            _____]

    3 - ( ) Don't know/unsure

——> [SKIP TO Q17] <——

Q13 Why haven't you ever made monetary donations to nonprofit organizations? [CHECK ALL THAT APPLY BELOW]

    1 - ( ) Cannot afford to

    2 - ( ) Don't know how the money is used by the nonprofits

    3 - ( ) Haven't found a cause I want to donate to

    4 - ( ) I donate to my church/synagogue and let them decide which nonprofits should receive the funds

    5 - ( ) Don't feel my donation could do much to help

    6 - ( ) Feel that these are obligations that the government should handle and fund

    7 - ( ) Other [SPECIFY: _____]

    8 - ( ) Never thought to donate

    9 - ( ) Don't know/unsure

(Continued)

Exhibit C-2 (Continued)

Q14 Is there anything that would encourage you to donate to a nonprofit organization?

    1 - ( ) Yes [SPECIFY: _____

    _____

    _____]

    2 - ( ) No [SPECIFY WHY NOT: _____

    _____

    _____]

    3 - ( ) Don't know/unsure

Q15 If you *were* to donate to nonprofit organizations, what type(s) would you most likely donate to? [CHECK ALL THAT APPLY]

    1 - ( ) Medical research

    2 - ( ) AIDs-related

    3 - ( ) Community service (general)

    4 - ( ) Food banks

    5 - ( ) Homeless shelters

    6 - ( ) Crisis centers

    7 - ( ) Childcare for low-income/single parent households

    8 - ( ) Religious-affiliated organizations

    9 - ( ) Arts-related organizations

    10 - ( ) Other [SPECIFY: _____]

    11 - ( ) Not applicable/would not donate regardless ——> [SKIP TO Q17]

    12 - ( ) Don't know/unsure ——> [SKIP TO Q17]

Q16 If you were to make a donation to a nonprofit organization, how would you prefer to make the donation? [CHECK ONE ONLY BELOW; MOST PREFERRED METHOD]

    1 - ( ) Cash

    2 - ( ) Personal check

    3 - ( ) Cashier's check/money order

(Continued)

Exhibit C–2 (Continued)

4 - ( ) Credit card

5 - ( ) Pledge and make payment on billing schedule

6 - ( ) Automatic deduction from paycheck

7 - ( ) Other [SPECIFY: _____]

8 - ( ) No preference

9 - ( ) Don't know/unsure

Q17 Have you ever done any volunteer work for any nonprofit organization? [NOTE THAT VOLUNTEER WORK INCLUDES ANY WORK DONE ON FUND-RAISERS, ETC.]

    1 - ( ) Yes ——> [CONTINUE TO Q18]

    2 - ( ) No ——> [SKIP TO Q23]

Q18 What type of volunteer work did you do?

_____

_____

_____

Q19 And for what organization(s) did you do this volunteer work?

_____

_____

_____

Q20 Why specifically did you select the organization(s) you volunteered for? [CHECK ALL THAT APPLY BELOW]

    1 - ( ) Heard about organization(s) through friend/family member

    2 - ( ) Once utilized their services

    3 - ( ) Heard of fund-raiser

    4 - ( ) Saw TV ad

    5 - ( ) Saw item about them on the news

    6 - ( ) Read article about them in newspaper

(Continued)

Exhibit C–2 (Continued)

7 - ( ) Saw solicitation for volunteers in newspaper

8 - ( ) Heard about them on the radio

9 - ( ) Heard solicitation for volunteers on radio

10 - ( ) My employer encourages volunteers there

11 - ( ) Other [SPECIFY: _____]

12 - ( ) Don't recall/unsure

Q21 How often do you do volunteer work with the organization(s) you mentioned above? [GIVE AVERAGE TIME FOR ALL ORGANIZATIONS COMBINED. CHECK ONE ONLY]

1 - ( ) Daily

2 - ( ) Several times per week

3 - ( ) Once a week

4 - ( ) Several times per month

5 - ( ) Once a month

6 - ( ) Once every couple of months

7 - ( ) A few times per year

8 - ( ) Once a year

9 - ( ) Other [SPECIFY: _____]

10 - ( ) Don't know/difficult to estimate

Q22 Is there anything that the organization(s) you volunteer with could do to encourage you to volunteer more often?

1 - ( ) Yes [SPECIFY: _____

_____

_____]

2 - ( ) No [SPECIFY WHY NOT: _____

_____

_____]

3 - ( ) Don't know/unsure

——> [SKIP TO Q27] <——

(Continued)

Exhibit C-2 (Continued)

Q23 Why haven't you ever done volunteer work for nonprofit organizations? [CHECK ALL THAT APPLY]

   1 - ( ) Don't have enough time

   2 - ( ) Hadn't ever considered it/thought of it

   3 - ( ) Have children/can't get away to do so

   4 - ( ) Don't know what I could do that would help

   5 - ( ) Have never been asked

   6 - ( ) Live too far from any of the nonprofits in my area

   7 - ( ) Prefer to donate money instead

   8 - ( ) Don't have transportation

   9 - ( ) Don't want to do volunteer work

  10 - ( ) Other [SPECIFY: _____]

  11 - ( ) Don't know/unsure

Q24 Is there anything that would encourage you to do volunteer work?

   1 - ( ) Yes [SPECIFY: _____

                                               ]

   2 - ( ) No [SPECIFY WHY NOT: _____

                                               ]

   3 - ( ) Don't know/unsure

Q25 If you were to do volunteer work, what type of nonprofit organization(s) would you be likely to get involved with? [CHECK ALL THAT APPLY]

   1 - ( ) AIDs-related

   2 - ( ) Hospices

   3 - ( ) Community service (general)

   4 - ( ) Childcare

   5 - ( ) Drug prevention

(Continued)

Exhibit C–2 (Continued)

6 - ( ) Homeless shelters

7 - ( ) Food banks

8 - ( ) Crisis center

9 - ( ) Religious affiliated charity

10 - ( ) Arts-related nonprofit

11 - ( ) Other [SPECIFY: _____]

12 - ( ) Not applicable/would not volunteer regardless ——> [SKIP TO Q27]

13 - ( ) Don't know/unsure

Q26 If you were to volunteer, what type of skills would you offer? [CHECK ALL THAT APPLY]

1 - ( ) Read/speak second language

2 - ( ) Clerical skills

3 - ( ) Personal computer skills

4 - ( ) Background in early childcare/education

5 - ( ) Medical skills

6 - ( ) Ability to drive vehicle/chauffeur

7 - ( ) Music

8 - ( ) Arts

9 - ( ) Skilled trades (i.e., carpentry, plumbing, electrician, etc.)

10 - ( ) Other [SPECIFY: _____]

11 - ( ) Don't know/unsure

Q27 Does anyone in your household volunteer?

1 - ( ) Yes

2 - ( ) No

Q28 Do you watch television three or more times per week?

1 - ( ) Yes ——> [CONTINUE TO Q29]

2 - ( ) No ——> [SKIP TO Q32]

(Continued)

Exhibit C–2 (Continued)

Q29 What channels do you typically watch?

_____

_____

_____

Q30 And when you watch television, what *types* of shows do you most often watch? [CHECK ALL THAT APPLY]

1 - ( ) Sitcoms

2 - ( ) Sports

3 - ( ) Movies (network)

4 - ( ) Cable movies/programs

5 - ( ) News

6 - ( ) Game shows

7 - ( ) Soap operas

8 - ( ) Other [SPECIFY: _____]

Q31 When do you usually watch television? [CHECK ALL THAT APPLY]

1 - ( ) Early morning

2 - ( ) Mid-morning

3 - ( ) Early afternoon

4 - ( ) Late afternoon

5 - ( ) Early evening

6 - ( ) Primetime

7 - ( ) Late night

8 - ( ) Other [SPECIFY: _____]

9 - ( ) Varies a lot

10 - ( ) Don't know/unsure

Q32 Do you listen to the radio at least once a day?

1 - ( ) Yes ——> [CONTINUE TO Q33]

2 - ( ) No ——> [SKIP TO Q36]

(Continued)

Exhibit C-2 (Continued)

Q33 What stations do you listen to most often?

_____

_____

_____

Q34 What types of radio programming do you prefer? [CHECK ALL THAT APPLY]

    1 - ( ) '90s rock

    2 - ( ) Easy listening

    3 - ( ) Oldies

    4 - ( ) Jazz/R&B

    5 - ( ) New age

    6 - ( ) Country

    7 - ( ) Talk radio

    8 - ( ) News

    9 - ( ) Other [SPECIFY: _____]

    10 - ( ) Varies a lot

    11 - ( ) Don't know/unsure

Q35 When do you usually listen to the radio? [CHECK ALL THAT APPLY]

    1 - ( ) Early morning

    2 - ( ) Morning commute-time

    3 - ( ) Mid-late morning

    4 - ( ) Lunchtime

    5 - ( ) Early afternoon

    6 - ( ) Mid-late afternoon

    7 - ( ) Afternoon commute-time

    8 - ( ) Early evening

    9 - ( ) Late evening

    10 - ( ) Other [SPECIFY: _____]

    11 - ( ) Don't know/unsure

(Continued)

Exhibit C–2 (Continued)

Q36 Do you read the newspaper at least three times per week?

    1 - ( ) Yes ——> [CONTINUE TO Q37]

    2 - ( ) No ——> [SKIP TO Q39]

Q37 Which papers do you usually read?

_____

_____

_____

Q38 Do you typically read specific sections, skim to find what interests you, or read the entire paper? [CHECK ONE ONLY BELOW]

    1 - ( ) Specific sections [SPECIFY: _____

    _____]

    2 - ( ) Skim the paper

    3 - ( ) Read the entire paper

    4 - ( ) Depends on the day/how much time I have

    5 - ( ) Don't know/unsure

Q39 Do you regularly commute to work or school?

    1 - ( ) Yes ——> [CONTINUE TO Q40]

    2 - ( ) No ——> [SKIP TO Q43]

Q40 How do you most often commute? [CHECK ONE ONLY—THE MOST USED METHOD]

    1 - ( ) Auto (alone)

    2 - ( ) Car/vanpool

    3 - ( ) Bus

    4 - ( ) Subway

    5 - ( ) Bike

    6 - ( ) Other [SPECIFY: _____]

    7 - ( ) Use combination of above methods

(Continued)

Exhibit C-2 (Continued)

8 - ( ) Depends on the day/weather/etc.

9 - ( ) Don't know/unsure

Q41 How many minutes would you say you spend on your commute on an average day? [PLEASE GIVE BEST ESTIMATE]

Minutes on Commute: ____ ____ ____ minutes

Q42 Do you ever read billboards or transit advertising (e.g., signs on buses) when you are commuting? [CHECK ONE ONLY BELOW]

1 - ( ) Yes, always

2 - ( ) Yes, occasionally

3 - ( ) No, never

4 - ( ) Don't know/unsure

Q43 Do you ever read direct mail advertisements or notices which you receive in your mail? [CHECK ONE ONLY BELOW]

1 - ( ) Yes, always

2 - ( ) Yes, occasionally

3 - ( ) No, never

4 - ( ) Don't know/unsure

The final series of questions is asked to allow your responses to be combined with those from other respondents with backgrounds similar to your own. Again, your responses will be kept confidential at all times.

Q44 Into which of the following age categories do you fall?

1 - ( ) 16–17

2 - ( ) 18–20

3 - ( ) 21–30

4 - ( ) 31–40

5 - ( ) 41–50

6 - ( ) 51–60

7 - ( ) Over 60

(Continued)

Exhibit C–2 (Continued)

Q45 And what was the last level of formal education which you had the opportunity to complete? [CHECK ONE ONLY]

  1 - ( ) Some high school or less

  2 - ( ) High school degree

  3 - ( ) Some college

  4 - ( ) 2-year college degree

  5 - ( ) 4-year college degree

  6 - ( ) Some trade school

  7 - ( ) Finished trade school

  8 - ( ) Some graduate school

  9 - ( ) Post-graduate degree

 10 - ( ) Other [SPECIFY: _____]

Q46 Into which of the following categories did your personal income before taxes fall last year?

  1 - ( ) Less than $25,000

  2 - ( ) $25,000 to $35,000

  3 - ( ) $36,000 to $45,000

  4 - ( ) $46,000 to $55,000

  5 - ( ) $56,000 to $75,000

  6 - ( ) Over $75,000

  7 - ( ) Don't know/unsure

Q47 How many dependents under the age of 18 do you personally have?

  1 - ( ) One

  2 - ( ) Two

  3 - ( ) Three or more

  4 - ( ) None

(Continued)

Exhibit C–2

Q48 Do you own or lease your home?

    1 - ( ) Own

    2 - ( ) Lease

    3 - ( ) Neither - live in someone else's home

    4 - ( ) Other [SPECIFY: _____]

Q49 What is your current occupation? [CHECK THE ONE BELOW WHICH BEST DESCRIBES YOUR OCCUPATION]

    1 - ( ) Clerical

    2 - ( ) Professional (Legal, Medical, etc.)

    3 - ( ) Middle Management

    4 - ( ) Blue collar

    5 - ( ) Skilled trades

    6 - ( ) Educator

    7 - ( ) Upper management/white collar

    8 - ( ) Small-business owner

    9 - ( ) Service-oriented (restaurant, hotel, airline, etc.)

    10 - ( ) Other [SPECIFY: _____]

Q50 Approximately how long have you been living in this area (*but not necessarily at this address*)?

    Time in Area: _____ Years/ _____ Months _____

Q51 What is your current home ZIP code?

    Home ZIP: _____

Q52 Please indicate your gender:

    1 - ( ) Female

    2 - ( ) Male

Thank you for your time and input! Please return your completed questionnaire in the return postage paid envelope that accompanied the survey packet.

Note that the outline simply provides a guideline. In reviewing the completed questionnaire, one can identify several areas where the questionnaire varies from the original survey outline. When actually developing the survey instrument, the Board discovered different ways to word questions that negated the need for other ones as well as identifying questions which were inadvertently left out of their original outline.

For example, a question was added which asks respondents who have made monetary donations to nonprofit organizations when they most recently had made such a donation. Rather than asking *why* nonvolunteers would select certain organizations to do volunteer work for, if this were to ever happen, the Board decided to identify the type of work they would be interested in volunteering for should the opportunity arise.

The entire section related to the effects of advertising was cut with the exception of a question concerning direct mail readership. The Board members felt that identifying what respondents read, view, and listen to would determine the best means of reaching them. If they were to ask about advertising effectiveness, answers might not be accurate and besides, nonprofit "ads" would not be comparable to those to which the respondents might refer. Finally, the Board also slipped in an additional demographic question as they had originally neglected to ask for respondents' genders.

Once the questionnaire was designed, the Board went through and, to cut the number of open-ended questions in the survey, developed precoded lists of area television channels, radio stations and newspapers, to provide respondents with a checklist and to cut down on coding efforts once the surveys were returned.

Analyzing the Results

The questionnaire was printed and mailed out to everyone on the sample which the Board of Directors had obtained. A cover letter was not sent with the survey in order to prevent connection of the study with City Lights. They did, however, add a survey deadline date to the end of the questionnaire in an attempt to ensure timely responses. While waiting for the completed questionnaires to be returned, one final task needed completion. They decided to hire a data processing firm to enter and process the results of the survey. First, this was much faster than doing it in-house. Second, it allowed them to honestly respond to donors, should the matter arise, that survey results were indeed kept confidential since they were tabulated by a disinterested third party. All that remained was for the Board to advise their vendor of the banner points (cross-tabulations) which they would require for the resulting data base tables. They decided to cross-tabulate all questions by gender, age categories, income categories, education level, number of years in the area (sorted by categories: "less than one year," "one to five years," "six to ten years," and "over ten years").

The survey deadline had allowed for four weeks of survey returns. This took into account the time it would take for respondents to receive their questionnaires, the time necessary to complete them and then the return mailing time. Given that the survey encompassed a fairly wide area, they wanted to allow plenty of time for the study. By their present deadline, there was a 12% survey response, with 603 completed surveys out of the 5,000 originally mailed out. Once the data was entered and processed, members received a set of data base tables. Each table represented responses to a single question asked in the survey and across the top of the table, banners indicated the cross-tabulation responses to each question.

Armed with these tables, the Board members evaluated the results of the survey, developed an executive summary report of the study, and made their recommendations for action. Given the survey results, they made the following recommendations:

- Most donors and potential donors would rather donate smaller amounts but more frequently during the year. Given this, a large-scale fund-raiser may not be the best means of encouraging donations. Rather City Lights will pursue an ongoing program to encourage donations regardless of the size but thereby creating the potential for a more loyal and regular donor base.

- The public is becoming more concerned that their donations are never actually reaching the people who need the money most. As a result they are either limiting their donations or carefully checking out those nonprofit organizations to whom they are donating their funds. To deal with these concerns, City Lights will make a concerted effort to get information to the public through the media as well as in its direct mail efforts which will clearly indicate how each dollar is distributed within the organization. Donors will also be given the option to designate whether they are donating to the organization's childcare center, homeless shelter, or crisis center.

- Nonvolunteers in the public sector are not volunteering time to nonprofit organizations mainly because they do not believe they have the time necessary. The organization will work to put in place a "telecommuter" version of volunteerism whereby certain clerical work, computer work, telephoning and counseling can be conducted from volunteers' homes. Applicants will be screened and interviewed as thoroughly as those for on-site volunteer work, but convenience to the volunteer will be heavily stressed.

- Many donors fall in the 16 to 20 age group. Board members recognize that this offers an opportunity to build strong and possibly life-long relationships with this group. The current corporate outreach program will be extended to cover schools, offering speakers, internships, scholarships and special donor programs in area high schools and colleges.

While these recommendations were based on the initial review of the results, the Board of Directors planned a follow-up meeting one month later to allow each member to have additional time to thoroughly read through the results again and to come back with any further comments or recommendations.

Case **Two**

The Electric Village

Identifying Research Needs

Fred Revson and Dave Edwards, co-owners of the Electric Village, a small, independent consumer electronics retail store, are concerned. An electronics "warehouse" superstore located just down the road will soon open its doors. Fred and Dave decide that they should conduct some (preferably inexpensive) research to prepare for the entry of this major competitor into their market, in particular to determine the impact on sales.

Determining Objectives

Fred and Dave had no problem identifying their main concerns and putting them into research objectives. They had never really spent time determining their market share in the surrounding area. Sales were steady although by no means outstanding, and they were not sure how they would be affected if the warehouse offered the substantially lower prices they are known for. Second, they were certain that their own service played a role in creating sales and repeat business but had not made an effort to verify this. Now, with the potential need for increased advertising, they needed to determine the most important issues to cover in their advertisements.

They needed to evaluate what attracted customers to them (as well as what attracted customers to competitors), and they needed to see if their strengths were being strongly contested by their competitors. Was their service exceptional (as they saw it), or were others offering the same service *plus* lower prices?

Thus their objectives were set as follows:

1. Determine current market share.
2. Determine factors used by consumers in selecting a consumer electronics store.
3. Identify the best means of competing with incoming competition.

Selecting Methodologies

While their objectives seemed simple enough at first glance, they required several different research methodologies to provide the information they required to make decisions. Determining market share was the item most easily dealt with. Assigned the secondary research, Fred (one of the owners) compiled sales information for the various consumer electronics stores and chains in the area, using recent figures provided by one of their industry trade associations. While some of the data was no doubt based on estimates, it still provided them with a good overview of where Electric Village stood prior to the entry of the new competitor in the market.

At the conclusion of this analysis, Ron estimated their market share to be approximately 11%, strong for a single independent store in a market where there had been a consistent influx of larger, recognized stores during the past two years.

Next Fred and Dave wanted to evaluate the factors considered by consumers when they are selecting a store where they will make consumer electronics purchases. Of course, the budget needs to be kept low. They discuss several survey methodologies. A mail survey won't provide quick results, but a phone survey will cost more than they have budgeted.

A very brief survey card placed at registers will provide information quickly and inexpensively. The cards can also be given to sales staff to ensure that all visitors are questioned regardless of whether or not they actually make a purchase. The first goal is to evaluate the competition and determine shoppers' reasons for coming to the Electric Village. Fred and Dave agreed that the goal was to get customers into the store. The survey card would ask questions related to how they heard of the store and what convinced them to come in and check it out. Similar questions would be asked to potential customers calling in to inquire about products, location, etc. If customers were willing, their names and addresses would also be included to allow the development of a mailing list to enhance their direct mail efforts.

The second phase was more time-consuming. In order to determine the best means of dealing with the continually increasing competition in their market, Fred and Dave settled on a mystery shop study. They arranged a trade-off with an area software store owner who attended many of the same industry-related events that they did throughout the year. Electric Village employees would shop the software stores in the area, while the software store staff would shop at area consumer electronics stores, including Electric Village, to evaluate prices, selection, service, and overall sales skills. Each company was responsible for developing its own evaluation form for the shops as well as for interpreting the results of the study once the completed forms were turned in. It was also agreed that, while the employees would be paid for hours incurred in the study, they would not know which of the stores they were "shopping" sponsored the mystery shop program.

Questionnaire/Evaluation Form Development

In-House Survey Cards

First, in order to get information coming in quickly, Fred designed a brief survey card. The idea was to maximize input while minimizing the customers' time being "wasted" while employees sought the answers. They simply needed to find out if this was the customer's first visit, first purchase, and the main reason they decided to come into the store. Identifying themselves and providing an address would be entirely optional, although politely requested, and a ZIP code would be obtained whenever possible. Fred and Dave agreed on the questions and did not need to outline such a brief questionnaire (Exhibit C–3).

Mystery Shop Evaluation Forms

The storeowners sat down and looked at issues which they believed needed to be evaluated in their upcoming mystery shop program. They were most interested in finding out about the *service* at competitors' stores, but also they wanted some insight regarding sales techniques. Fred and Dave emphasized fitting the right product to the customer along with offering weekly classes on programming your VCR, how to set up the perfect sound system, etc. Customers making purchases of $150 or more were given passes to a class of their choice. Typically they did not run major sales, but concentrated on making the purchase experience a convenient and pleasant one. Coffee was served in an area at the front of the store where customers were greeted by a salesperson. Sales staff were referred to as "tour guides," and they sat down with customers at the start to look through a catalogue of available products and to probe for the customers' needs. Then they took customers through the store to look at appropriate items in their price range. They would show the higher end items as well, however, noting where they were perceived as being superior. Then and only then was browsing encouraged. All large-sized items would be delivered free of charge.

The store owners were certain that their service level was unmatched in the area, but were also aware of the lure of lower prices in an economy where lay-offs were becoming the "norm." Therefore, they also decided to include price issues in their shops, at least in terms of how prices were "sold." They had actual price information as their employees went out weekly to do price comparisons.

To simplify the evaluation form design process, they decided to list the specific criteria that they wanted shoppers to rate:

- Salesperson's attitude
- Willingness to help customers

Exhibit C–3

Customer Information Card

Dear Customer: Please take a moment to give us your feedback on this particular visit to our store. Thank you!

Q1 Is this your first visit to our store?

    1 - Yes

    2 - No ——> [SPECIFY APPROXIMATE # PAST VISITS: _____]

Q2 Did you make a purchase today?

    1 - ( ) Yes, this was my first purchase at your store

    2 - ( ) Yes and I have purchased in the past

    3 - ( ) No, but I have purchased in the past

    4 - ( ) No and I have never purchased at your store

Q3 Please indicate your top three reasons for coming into the store today. Write 1, 2 and 3 next to the appropriate reasons, with 1 being the main reason for your decision and 2 and 3 your second and third most important reasons for that decision.

    _____ Convenient location

    _____ Recommendation from friend/family-member

    _____ Past purchase experience

    _____ Extended warranty program

    _____ Availability of financing

    _____ Low prices

    _____ In-house repair service

    _____ Education of customers

    _____ Good service

    _____ Return policy

    _____ Free delivery service

    _____ Knowledgeable sales staff

    _____ Other [SPECIFY: _____]

(Continued)

Exhibit C–3

Q4 Is there anything we would do to serve you better?

_____

_____

_____

Q5 What is your home ZIP code? ___ ___ ___ ___ ___

Thank you for your time and comments!

- Length of time customers wait for assistance
- Number of products actually *presented*
- Detail of presentation
- Probing for customers' needs
- Service options discussed (delivery, education, other)
- Mentions of/attitudes toward competitors
- Extended warranty offered
- General courtesy issues (shook hands, smiled, thanked customers for coming in)

Given that nonprofessional "shoppers" would be conducting the study, Fred and Dave decided to keep the evaluation form as simple as possible, concentrating only on these issues. They did not include parking issues or signage as they recognized that many of the competitors had advantages in those areas and, given their current location, they would not be able to make such changes at that time. (See Exhibit C–4.)

Fred and Dave added questions 15 and 16 knowing that their shoppers would be sales representatives themselves. They expected that this might give some added insight when their results came back in.

Exhibit C–4

Consumer Electronics Shop Evaluation Form

Date: ___ /___ /___ Start Time: ___ :___ AM/PM End Time: ___ :___ AM/PM

Shopper Name: _____ Store Name: _____

Store Address: _____

Sales Rep's Name: _____

****

Q1 When you entered the store, from the time you walked in the door, approximately how long did it take for a salesperson to greet you? [CHECK ONE ONLY]

    1 - ( ) No time at all/salesperson greeted me immediately

    2 - ( ) Less than one minute

    3 - ( ) One to three minutes

    4 - ( ) Four to six minutes

    5 - ( ) Seven to ten minutes

    6 - ( ) Eleven to fifteen minutes

    7 - ( ) Sixteen to twenty minutes

    8 - ( ) Over twenty minutes

Q2 On a scale of one to five (1 = "not at all inviting;" 5 = "very inviting") how would you rate this particular store in terms of how its interior appeared?

    CIRCLE ONE RATING ONLY: 1   2   3   4   5

    [IF GAVE "1" OR "2" PLEASE INDICATE WHY: _____

    _____

    _____

(Continued)

Exhibit C-4 (Continued)

Q3 Please indicate which of the following the sales representative did during the course of your visit: [CHECK ALL THAT DID OCCUR]

1 - ( ) Sales rep smiled

2 - ( ) Sales rep introduced him/herself

3 - ( ) Sales rep asked your name and used it

4 - ( ) Sales rep shook your hand

Q4 On a rating scale of one to five (1 = "poor"; 5 = "excellent"), please rate the sales representative who assisted you on how well she/he did performing the following sales-related skills: [CIRCLE ONE RATING PER ITEM]

(a) Asked questions to determine my needs

1   2   3   4   5

(b) Was willing to help me make the right choice

1   2   3   4   5

(c) Showed me several options that would meet my needs

1   2   3   4   5

(d) Gave details re each product presented (price, warranty, performance issues)

1   2   3   4   5

Q5 Overall, how many products did the representative present to you?

Products: _____

Q6 How much time did the representative spend with you discussing your needs and/or presenting products?

OVERALL TIME SPENT: _____ MINUTES

(Continued)

Exhibit C–4 (Continued)

Q7 Which of the following services/options were mentioned to you by the sales representative? [CHECK ALL THAT WERE MENTIONED]

    1 - ( ) Warranties on products

    2 - ( ) Delivery

    3 - ( ) Customer education

    4 - ( ) Installation

    5 - ( ) Return policies

Q8 Did the representative ever have to check with his manager/supervisor to get answers to your questions?

    1 - ( ) Yes [DESCRIBE SITUATION: _____

_____

_____]

    2 - ( ) No

Q9 At any time during your shop did the representative (or anyone else in the store) mention any competitors to you?

    1 - ( ) Yes ——> [CONTINUE TO Q10]

    2 - ( ) No ——> [SKIP TO Q12]

Q10 In what context were the comments made? [CHECK ALL THAT APPLY]

    1 - ( ) They did not have product/suggested a specific competitor

    2 - ( ) Noted that they (service/price/etc.) are better than a specific competitor

    3 - ( ) Suggested that the customer should compare prices and check a specific competitor

    4 - ( ) Suggested that a specific competitor was not "up to par" in terms of price, service, etc.)

    5 - ( ) Other [SPECIFY: _____]

(Continued)

Exhibit C–4 (Continued)

Q11 What competitors did they specifically name?

_____

_____

Q12 Based on your visit to this store, which of the following best describes how you would have reacted in "real life"? [CHECK ONE ONLY]

1 - ( ) Would have bought product right then

2 - ( ) Would have considered purchasing product, but would shop around first

3 - ( ) Would have tried to talk them down on price or get "extras" before buying

4 - ( ) Would not have purchased from this store/would definitely look elsewhere

Q13 Please explain your reasons for your response in Q12:

_____

_____

_____

_____

Q14 On a scale of one to five, (1 = "poor"; 5 = "excellent"), please rate this store on the following aspects, taking into consideration your entire shop experience today:

(a) Price	1	2	3	4	5
(b) Product Selection	1	2	3	4	5
(c) Sales Staff's Attitude	1	2	3	4	5
(d) Knowledge of Staff	1	2	3	4	5
(e) Quality of Service	1	2	3	4	5
(f) Availability of Added Benefits	1	2	3	4	5

(Continued)

Exhibit C-4

Q15 If you were looking for a new sales job, would you personally want to work at this particular store?

1 - ( ) Yes, definitely

2 - ( ) Possibly

3 - ( ) No, definitely not

Q16 Please explain your response to Q15:

_____

_____

_____

_____

ADDITIONAL COMMENTS:

_____

_____

_____

_____

A detailed shopper briefing was held at a neutral location. A friend of Dave's conducted the session to avoid anyone connecting the study with any specific consumer electronics store. Then shoppers were given a two-week period during which they could complete their assigned shops. Each area consumer electronics store was shopped twice for a total of 50 shops. These included shops of several major department store consumer electronics departments.

Evaluating the Results

The in-house survey yielded some interesting results for the store owners. Initial findings suggested that customers had heard that they had a reputation for good service and a knowledgeable sales staff. Far fewer than they had expected, however, were repeat customers. Second, while they appreciated the *staff* being knowledgeable, few were actually willing to attend an education class even if it was free! While these results were by no means a large enough sample to do heavy analysis on, they did provide input from a new perspective.

The mystery shop results also yielded some unexpected information. The competition was *not* as far behind in the service aspects as they had originally thought. Many were offering free delivery, and more were apparently encouraging sales representatives to spend a longer time with the customer to meet needs. Others, instead of offering classes to consumers, were providing that "training" when the product was set up *in their homes*. Instead of being at the "cutting edge" of service, Fred and Dave were actually falling a bit behind!

Given the results of their studies, they sat down and developed the following action points to work on in the coming year:

- Put the funds used in supporting consumer classes into additional sales staff training. Offer customers an extra $10 off any product totaling $50 or more if the sales representative cannot answer an operations, price or warranty-related question concerning that specific product.

- Develop a data base of customers: past ones, using sales information to input the data, and current ones, using the survey when possible. Use this information to offer specials to these customers or to announce upcoming events. This should help increase repeat business.

- Offer in-house set-up of all products from VCRs to big-screen TVs and include a 15-minute session with the customer explaining how to operate their new equipment.

- Comments also indicated that many customers found the immediate contact with a sales representative a bit intimidating. They liked to establish their own comfort level with the prices and products *before* someone started asking *them* questions. As a result, Fred and Dave planned to reverse their sales methods. They would leave the coffee and catalogues out for the customer to use as needed.

They would smile and greet customers and give them a business card and then "back off" for as long as the customer wanted. When the customer was ready to ask questions or to deal, he/she would take the card to the desk and the appropriate salesperson would be paged. *Then* the probing and assistance would take place. While the staff would be readily available, there would be less pressure on the customer, who would have the freedom to browse as would be allowed in the warehouse store atmosphere.

- Pricing would not be lowered to compete with the warehouse store as this would affect service standards. They would advertise on a service platform and emphasize the added convenience of staff knowledge, free delivery and in-house "education" with set-ups.

Fred and Dave anticipate that these moves will allow them to maintain their market share and possibly increase it despite the new store's entry into the market. They plan to keep a close eye on the incoming comment cards to identify possible fluctuations in their customer base and customers' needs. Should those arise, they will again attempt additional research to help them make their decisions. They also plan to conduct a second series of mystery shops to include the warehouse store once it has been in their market for about six months.

Case Three

Miller Floral Shops

Identifying Research Needs

Bill Miller, a florist who owned three locations in a large metropolitan area, wanted to develop stronger customer relationships and increase repeat business, but did not, however, know what specifically would encourage this. He had checked with industry resources and reviewed industry research, but felt that, since it was conducted several years earlier, it might be a bit out of date. He wanted to get a general feel for how he could build stronger relationships, but did not have specific lists of questions to ask consumers. Instead, he had a few ideas—in particular, an idea for a customer appreciation program—which he wanted to get feed-back on to determine if the concept would work in his market.

Determining Objectives

Miller sat down and listed what he would want to find out from his study and narrowed down his objectives to the following:

1. Determine factors involved in selecting a florist in an area for the first time.

2. Evaluate what makes a customer go back more than once to a florist.

3. Testing customer appreciation program options.

He felt he knew *when* people make purchases and for what occasions, but he wanted to find out what determined customer loyalty—what makes customers change florists or continue with one specific florist. He also wanted to test his ideas about a customer appreciation program on both current and prospective customers to see if it could potentially have the desired effect.

Selecting a Methodology

Given the fact that Bill needed to *test* several concepts with consumers, focus groups seemed to be the best methodology to meet his stated objectives. He decided to hold two focus groups, one of customers who had been to his shop *once only* during the past six months and one of floral purchasers who had *not* been to his shop within the past two years. Based on his time restraints, he chose to use a local research vendor, who, in addition to providing the facility, would handle recruiting, taping, and moderating. To keep costs to a minimum, however, he would draft screener questionnaires, provide lists of *his* customers for recruiting purposes, draft a moderator's guide, and do his own evaluation of the group results.

Developing Screeners/Moderator's Guide

Miller identified those items which would need to be "screened" when recruiting participants for his focus groups:

- Last purchase of flowers through his shop (customers) / through other shops (noncustomers).
- Ensuring that recruits don't work for any florist.

Given this information he developed the focus group screener shown in Exhibit C–5.

The research vendor began recruiting participants for the two focus groups and meanwhile Miller drafted a moderator's discussion guide based on the information he wanted to obtain (Exhibit C–6).

Exhibit C–5

Focus Group Screener

DATE: _____ PHONE: (___) ___-____

INTERVIEWER: _____ CUSTOMER: 1 - YES 2 - NO

****

[ASK TO SPEAK TO HEAD OF HOUSEHOLD 18 YEARS OF AGE OR OLDER]

Hello, my name is _____ , calling from **ABC** Research. We are conducting a brief study concerning purchases of floral products. This will only take a few minutes and your responses will be kept confidential.

Q1 Have you purchased cut flowers or floral arrangements within the past two years?

    1 - ( ) Yes ——> [CONTINUE TO Q2]

    2 - ( ) No ——> [THANK & TERMINATE]

    3 - ( ) Don't recall ——> [THANK & TERMINATE]

Q2 Have you ever purchased flowers at Miller Floral Shop?

    1 - ( ) Yes ——> [CONTINUE TO Q3]

    2 - ( ) No ——> [SKIP TO Q4]

Q3 Have you purchased flowers at Miller's more than once within the past six months?

    1 - ( ) Yes ——> [THANK & TERMINATE]

    2 - ( ) No ——> [SKIP TO Q5]

Q4 We will be conducting a focus group discussion on Wednesday, March 6th, at 6 P.M. to discuss floral purchasing habits. Refreshments will be served and you will receive $30 for your participation. There will be no

(Continued)

Exhibit C–5

sales effort and we would appreciate your input. The group will last about 90 minutes. Will you be able to join us?

1 - ( ) Yes - - -> [NOTE NAME/ADDRESS TO SEND DIRECTIONS]

2 - ( ) No - - -> [THANK & TERMINATE]

****

Q5 We will be conducting a focus group discussion on Wednesday, March 6th, at 8 P.M. to discuss floral purchasing habits. Refreshments will be served and you will receive $30 for your participation. There will be no sales effort, and we would appreciate your input. The group will last about 90 minutes. Will you be able to join us?

1 - ( ) Yes ——> [GET NAME/ADDRESS TO SEND DIRECTIONS]

2 - ( ) No ——> [THANK & TERMINATE]

****

NAME: _____

ADDRESS: _____

Exhibit C-6

Focus Group Discussion Guide

(10 Mins.)   INTRODUCTION

- Greeting
- Purpose of Focus Group - to discuss floral purchasing habits
- Role of Moderator
- Recording the Groups
- Confidentiality of Comments

(20 Mins.)   FLORAL PURCHASING HABITS

- What occasions do you buy flowers/floral items for?
    - Send alone or with card/other items (i.e., toys/balloons/candy)?
- Typically wire orders, carry-out or local delivery?
- Average amount spent per order?
- Number of purchases per year?
- Preferred floral items (cut, in vase, arranged, boxed, other)?
- Where flowers are typically bought?

(20 Mins.)   VENDOR DECISIONS

- Why do you buy flowers from [RESPONSES ABOVE]?
- How do you decide where to purchase flowers?
  [PROMPT: ADS, YELLOW PAGES, PAST EXPERIENCE, LOCATION, RECOMMENDATIONS]
- Most important of these factors in making your decision?
    - Price
    - Quality
    - Location
    - Reputation
    - Familiarity

(Continued)

Exhibit C–6

(30 Mins.)   TESTING CUSTOMER APPRECIATION PROGRAM

- Ever go back to same place to purchase flowers?
  - Why?
  - Why not?
- What would encourage you to go back more often to one florist?
- Familiar with any type of retail customer appreciation program?
  - Interested in one for a florist?
- Ask interest levels for each of following possible program aspects:
  - Frequent purchaser point program
  - Discounts on special holiday items
  - Free local delivery on purchases over $15
  - Seminars in flower arranging/gardening
  - In-shop records of your family members'/friends' birthdays and anniversaries with reminder cards to you with discount coupons
  - Other suggestions?
  - What would requirements be to be included in the program?

    [PROMPT: X NUMBER OF PURCHASES, $100 IN PURCHASES IN A QUARTER, ETC.]

(10 Mins.)   CLOSING COMMENTS

Analysis of the Results

Using the discussion guide (Exhibit C–6), ABC Research conducted Miller's focus groups, including videotaping. Upon review of the tapes he determined that most floral purchasers send flowers because they feel it is a fast, convenient way to meet obligations. However, they are price conscious and look for the best price on both the item ordered and the delivery fee. His concept of a customer appreciation program was welcomed, but with some revisions. Most were interested in any of the items that saved them money, and felt that there should be a free delivery benefit for wire orders as well. They suggested that they would like verification of delivery so they would not have to ask the recipient if it got there. They were not particularly interested in having seminars offered, but they did like the idea of having an in-house record to remind them of upcoming birthdays and anniversaries. The participants agreed that they would definitely return to one florist on a regular basis given these benefits. As a result, Miller began setting up this program in his shops, beginning by having ABC Research send the participants several coupons to try his shop out in the near future!

Glossary

Banner Headings used in data tables of survey results

Base Total number of responses to a given survey question; also the total number of completed surveys or shops in a research project

Bid A written proposal from a research vendor, including costs, submitted in response to an RFP

Briefing An interviewer training session specifically related to a new survey or study

Cannibalization In a marketing sense, a firm losing customers from one of its locations to another

Clarification Asking respondents to further define their responses, such as stating a complete name versus an acronym

Closed-ended questions Questions that require specific responses to be selected, such as "yes" or "no," one or more of several possible multiple-choice responses, or a numerical rating

Coding The process of reviewing all of the verbatim responses to a given question and grouping like responses for analysis

Confidence level The level or percentage of confidence you need to have that your survey results will fall within a specific range of reliability

Confirmation letter Letter sent to persons recruited for a focus group to provide directions to the group and serve as a reminder of the time and date of the group

Co-op fees Payment made to focus group participants, usually in the form of cash

Cross-tabulate To tabulate responses to survey questions by the responses given to another selected question such as age, gender, or income level

Demographic questions Questions about respondents, such as age, income, education level, gender, and ethnic background, typically used in cross-tabs to provide more meaningful analysis of survey results

Editing A careful review of completed questionnaires to ensure that all skip patterns and indicated instructions have been followed correctly

Efficiencies of scale Cost savings that arise from combining the operations or expenses of two divisions, purchasing in larger quantities, etc.

Flowchart A visual diagram used in questionnaire design that indicates each survey question and its related skip pattern

Focus group A research discussion group conducted by a moderator and designed to create an ongoing conversation about one or more issues related to a general topic

Focus group room Typically a large conference room with a one-way mirror to allow for videotaping and client viewing of the group(s)

Incentive A form of compensation provided if a person responds as requested to a survey or otherwise participates in a research study

Incidence rate The percentage of qualified respondents within a given population

Intercept interviews A research method in which interviewers stop consumers on the street or in a mall to conduct in-person interviews

List broker Firm that sells lists covering an extensive variety of detailed breakdowns such as geographic location, age, profession, etc.

Market research The process of gathering and analyzing information about the market in order to provide information for decision making

Methodology The means by which a study is conducted (e.g., mail surveys, mystery shops, focus groups)

Moderator's discussion guide An outline used by a focus group moderator to assist in conducting the discussion in an orderly manner and to ensure that all necessary topics are covered during the group

Monitoring Listening to survey interviews to verify that interviewers are conducting the survey correctly and that respondents are correctly interpreting the questions being asked

Multiple-response questions Questions that allow respondents to select one or more responses to the questions

Mystery shops Studies in which interviewers go into an establishment under guise of being customers or potential customers to test that company's service and sales efforts

Nonresponse rate Percentage of contacts on the sample list that do not respond to a survey

One-on-one interviews Less structured "surveys" or discussions conducted in person by an interviewer with one participant at a time

Open-ended questions Questions that allow respondents to write out or respond with detailed answers in their own words

Population The overall group from which a survey's sample is selected

Pretest A "trial run," usually of a telephone survey, consisting of approximately 10–20 interviews to test the length of the survey, question wording, etc.

Primary research Research designed specifically to address the research objective(s) currently being considered

Probing Process by which interviewers encourage survey respondents to elaborate on their responses

Qualify To determine through screening questions whether a respondent is the correct person to participate in a study (e.g., the head of the household, 18 years of age or older, etc.)

Qualitative research Less structured research methods (e.g., focus groups or one-on-one interviews) whose results are open to subjective interpretation

Quantitative research Structured research methods designed to provide statistically valid results in the form of numbers and percentages

Questionnaire A survey instrument designed to gather data in a research survey by posing pertinent questions to respondents by phone or mail

Quotas Preassigned segments of survey sample to be interviewed, such as 50 percent females and 50 percent males

Ranking questions Questions that ask respondents to place a number of items in order by importance, preference, etc.

Rating questions Questions that ask respondents to assign values (or ratings) from a predetermined scale to a series of items or statements

Recruiting The process of qualifying and inviting contacts to participate in a focus group

Request for proposal (RFP) A formal letter to research vendors identifying research needs and asking them to respond with recommended methodologies and estimated pricing

Research objectives What it is that the researcher wants to find out from the research study

Research vendor A professional research company typically offering a variety of market research services, including focus groups, surveys, and mystery shop programs

Respondent A person who completes a questionnaire by phone or mail

RFP See **Request for proposal**

Sample The lists of people or businesses who will be contacted to participate in a given study

Scale A specified range of numbers assigned to qualitative terms to allow numerical assessment of a quality or issue

Scenarios Predetermined situations used by mystery shoppers to evaluate staff reactions

Screener questionnaire Brief questionnaire used to recruit participants for focus groups or one-on-one interviews

Screening questions Questions asked to ensure that survey respondents meet qualifications for the sample

Secondary research Gathering data that was compiled previously by another organization or internally for a different research objective

Single-response questions Questions that allow respondents to give only one possible response

Skip pattern Part of a questionnaire's format such that, if a certain response is given, the respondent is asked to jump ahead, or "skip" to a specified question

Survey Research study using a questionnaire to collect data from respondents via telephone or mail contact

Survey sampling The process of using specific criteria to select a group of contacts to be surveyed

Tabulate To tally survey responses

Target market The segment of the market or the group of potential customers to which sales efforts are directed

Validate To call back a respondent and repeat key survey questions to ascertain that interviewers are correctly recording responses

Index

American Marketing Association

As a marketing professional or student you'll never get enough information about marketing.

One way to stay up-to-date with the latest academic theories, the war stories, the global techniques, and the leading technologies is to become a member of the American Marketing Association.

For a free membership information kit
phone: 312-648-0536,
FAX: 312-993-7542,
or write to the American Marketing Association at 250 S. Wacker Drive, Chicago, Illinois, 60606.

TITLES OF INTEREST IN MARKETING, DIRECT MARKETING, AND SALES PROMOTION

SUCCESSFUL DIRECT MARKETING METHODS, by Bob Stone
PROFITABLE DIRECT MARKETING, by Jim Kobs
INTEGRATED DIRECT MARKETING, by Ernan Roman
BEYOND 2000: THE FUTURE OF DIRECT MARKETING, by Jerry I. Reitman
POWER DIRECT MARKETING, by "Rocket" Ray Jutkins
CREATIVE STRATEGY IN DIRECT MARKETING, by Susan K. Jones
SECRETS OF SUCCESSFUL DIRECT MAIL, by Richard V. Benson
STRATEGIC DATABASE MARKETING, by Rob Jackson and Paul Wang
SUCCESSFUL TELEMARKETING, by Bob Stone and John Wyman
BUSINESS TO BUSINESS DIRECT MARKETING, by Robert Bly
COMMONSENSE DIRECT MARKETING, by Drayton Bird
DIRECT MARKETING CHECKLISTS, by John Stockwell and Henry Shaw
INTEGRATED MARKETING COMMUNICATIONS, by Don E. Schultz, Stanley I. Tannenbaum,
    and Robert F. Lauterborn
NEW DIRECTIONS IN MARKETING, by Aubrey Wilson
GREEN MARKETING, by Jacquelyn Ottman
MARKETING CORPORATE IMAGE: THE COMPANY AS YOUR NUMBER ONE PRODUCT, by James R. Gregory
    with Jack G. Wiechmann
HOW TO CREATE SUCCESSFUL CATALOGS, by Maxwell Sroge
101 TIPS FOR MORE PROFITABLE CATALOGS, by Maxwell Sroge
SALES PROMOTION ESSENTIALS, by Don E. Schultz, William A. Robinson and Lisa A. Petrison
PROMOTIONAL MARKETING, by William A. Robinson and Christine Hauri
BEST SALES PROMOTIONS, by William A. Robinson
INSIDE THE LEADING MAIL ORDER HOUSES, by Maxwell Sroge
NEW PRODUCT DEVELOPMENT, by George Gruenwald
NEW PRODUCT DEVELOPMENT CHECKLISTS, by George Gruenwald
CLASSIC FAILURES IN PRODUCT MARKETING, by Donald W. Hendon
HOW TO TURN CUSTOMER SERVICE INTO CUSTOMER SALES, by Bernard Katz
ADVERTISING & MARKETING CHECKLISTS, by Ron Kaatz
BRAND MARKETING, by William M. Weilbacher
MARKETING WITHOUT MONEY, by Nicholas E. Bade
THE 1-DAY MARKETING PLAN, by Roman A. Hiebing, Jr. and Scott W. Cooper
HOW TO WRITE A SUCCESSFUL MARKETING PLAN, by Roman G. Hiebing, Jr. and Scott W. Cooper
DEVELOPING, IMPLEMENTING, AND MANAGING EFFECTIVE MARKETING PLANS, by Hal Goetsch
HOW TO EVALUATE AND IMPROVE YOUR MARKETING DEPARTMENT, by Keith Sparling and Gerard Earls
SELLING TO A SEGMENTED MARKET, by Chester A. Swenson
MARKET-ORIENTED PRICING, by Michael Morris and Gene Morris
STATE-OF-THE-ART MARKETING RESEARCH, by A.B. Blankenship and George E. Breen
AMA HANDBOOK FOR CUSTOMER SATISFACTION, by Alan Dutka
WAS THERE A PEPSI GENERATION BEFORE PEPSI DISCOVERED IT?, by Stanley C. Hollander
    and Richard Germain
BUSINESS TO BUSINESS COMMUNICATIONS HANDBOOK, by Fred Messner
MANAGING SALES LEADS: HOW TO TURN EVERY PROSPECT INTO A CUSTOMER, by Robert Donath,
    Richard Crocker, Carol Dixon and James Obermeyer
AMA MARKETING TOOLBOX (SERIES), by David Parmerlee
AMA COMPLETE GUIDE TO SMALL BUSINESS MARKETING, by Kenneth J. Cook
AMA COMPLETE GUIDE TO STRATEGIC PLANNING FOR SMALL BUSINESS, by Kenneth J. Cook
AMA COMPLETE GUIDE TO SMALL BUSINESS ADVERTISING, by Joe Vitale
HOW TO GET THE MOST OUT OF TRADE SHOWS, by Steve Miller
HOW TO GET THE MOST OUT OF SALES MEETINGS, by James Dance
STRATEGIC MARKET PLANNING, by Robert J. Hamper and L. Sue Baugh

For further information or a current catalog, write:
NTC Business Books
a division of NTC Publishing Group
4255 West Touhy Avenue
Lincolnwood, Illinois 60646–1975 U.S.A.